The Screwtape Letters

ALSO AVAILABLE FROM HARPERONE

The Signature Classics:
Mere Christianity
The Screwtape Letters
The Great Divorce
The Problem of Pain
Miracles
A Grief Observed
The Abolition of Man
The Weight of Glory
George MacDonald: An Anthology

A Year with C. S. Lewis
Yours, Jack
Words to Live By
A Year with Aslan

ALSO AVAILABLE FROM HARPERCOLLINS

The Chronicles of Narnia:
The Magician's Nephew
The Lion, the Witch, and the Wardrobe
The Horse and His Boy
Prince Caspian
The Voyage of the Dawn Treader
The Silver Chair
The Last Battle

The Screwtape Letters

and

SCREWTAPE PROPOSES A TOAST

ANNOTATED EDITION

C. S. LEWIS

with annotations by Paul McCusker

HarperOne
An Imprint of HarperCollinsPublishers

HarperOne

FIRST EDITION

Designed by Ralph Fowler

Library of Congress Cataloging-in-Publication Data is available upon request.

ISBN 978-0-06-202317-9

14 15 16 17   RRD(H)   10 9 8 7 6 5 4 3 2

TO J. R. R. TOLKIEN

Best known as the author of *The Hobbit* and *The Lord of the Rings,* John Ronald Reuel Tolkien (1892–1973) was a close friend to C. S. Lewis and fellow member of a discussion group called The Inklings, in which members read their works to each other. Lewis credited Tolkien as having been instrumental in his conversion to Christianity in 1931. Tolkien credited Lewis with providing the encouragement to finish and publish *The Lord of the Rings*. This dedication would have come during a peak period in their friendship.

Contents

Introduction to the Annotated Edition

While working on a dramatization of *The Screwtape Letters* for Focus on the Family's *Radio Theatre,* I became aware of two things. First, *The Screwtape Letters* is as relevant to the twenty-first century as it was to the twentieth. Second, though *Screwtape* is timeless in its perspectives, the writing *is* fixed in time and many of the references, words, and phrases have been lost to the generations since it was written. So I put it to Douglas Gresham, Lewis's stepson, that someone ought to do an annotated version to help modern readers along.

He hated the idea. For him, the authors of annotated books too often try to interpret the material for the audience—and often get it wrong. I assured him that it was possible for an annotated edition to illuminate the material without attempting to interpret it. I believed that for readers to understand the classic works of literature or philosophical concepts Lewis referenced, as well as how Lewis explored ideas in his other works, they would have a richer experience with *The Screwtape Letters.*

To that, he agreed. And he gave me the honor of taking on the effort, though I am not, nor have I ever pretended to be, an academic. That wasn't important to him. He wanted *The Screwtape Letters* to be accessible to as broad an audience as possible.

With that said, I should be clear that this book is *not* an interpretation of *The Screwtape Letters* nor of C. S. Lewis. Apart from the mandate from Doug Gresham himself, I wouldn't attempt such a thing. Greater minds than mine have debated this work and its meanings since the book's release. I have no interest in adding my opinions to the debate.

And I'm sensitive that Lewis himself loathed the practice of poring over an author's life to discern some deep, inner meaning to a written work. In a letter dated January 19, 1948, Lewis wrote to the Reverend Roy W. Harrington in answer to a request for some background material about his life. Lewis stated, "The only thing of any importance (if that is) about me is what

I have to say." He went on to explain one of his favorite "peeves":

> I can't abide the idea that a man's books should be "set in their biographical context" and if I had some rare information about the private life of Shakespeare or Dante I'd throw it in the fire, tell no one, and re-read their works. All this biographical interest is only a device for indulging in gossip as an excuse for not reading what the chaps say, [which] is their only real claim on our attention. (I here resist a wild impulse to invent some really exciting background—that I am an illegitimate son of Edward VII, married to a chimpanzee, was rescued from the practice of magic by a Russian monk, and always eat eggs with the shells on.)[1]

Yet Lewis himself, as a teacher of English literature, understood the importance of putting a work and its author into its historical context. His *English Literature in the Sixteenth Century* and *The Discarded Image* are only two of many examples where he does that very thing.

1. C. S. Lewis, *The Collected Letters of C. S. Lewis, Vol. II: Books, Broadcasts, and the War 1931–1949*, edited by Walter Hooper (San Francisco: HarperCollins, 2004).

It was a tribute to his audience that Lewis never spoke down to them. He seemed to assume that his readers were as well read as he was. Perhaps they were then. Now, however, annotations are needed to help contemporary readers who haven't been educated to the high standards of Oxford or Cambridge in 1941, or who know little or nothing about the world in which Lewis wrote.

Also buried in *The Screwtape Letters* are themes and ideas that Lewis had touched on in earlier works or would develop more fully later. For example, the phrase "merely Christian" is used by Screwtape in "Letter 25" to describe Christians who embrace a "mere Christianity"—as opposed to Screwtape's preferred "Christianity *and . . .*" The concept of "mere Christianity" was actually explored long before Lewis adopted the phrase, as you'll see in the annotation. And Lewis would later develop "mere Christianity" in a series of "broadcast talks" he did for the BBC.[2] Those talks became his classic book *Mere Christianity.* That's one example of how I hope these annotations will help.

Finally, in some cases, Lewis uses words and phrases that have fallen out of use or have changed meaning over the years, or over the Atlantic. Where possible, I give a simple explanation of what those words or phrases mean.

With all that said, my greatest hope is that the reader will find in this edition even more reasons to love and appreciate Lewis's brilliant classic.

The Context for Screwtape

By the time C. S. Lewis had the spark of an idea for *The Screwtape Letters* in 1940, the world around him was changing dramatically.

In July, Germany's war against Britain had taken to the skies as the German Luftwaffe hoped to decimate the Royal Air Force over the English Channel. Then, in September, the Germans changed their strategy and began bombing England's cities. London was the main target. By the end of that month alone, over seven thousand people had been killed and nine thousand injured. The Blitz, as it was known, would last until May 1941 and would pervade Lewis's consciousness while writing *The Screwtape Letters*.

That period would also prove to be a remarkable time for Lewis's career. He was commissioned by publisher Ashley Sampson to contribute a book to the Christian Challenge series. The subject was "pain." And from that commission came *The Problem of Pain,* published in the autumn of 1940.

The Problem of Pain was critically acclaimed, and Lewis was acclaimed for tackling such a difficult subject with honesty and clarity of thought. The book came to the attention of James Welch, the director of the BBC's Religious Broadcasting department. On February 7, 1941, Welch wrote to Lewis with a couple of suggestions about a series of radio broadcasts they might produce together. An exchange of letters followed, leading to four broadcast talks given by Lewis called *Right and Wrong as a Clue to the Meaning of the Universe.* The following year he would write two more series and in 1944 yet another. Not long after that, all four efforts would wind up as the published *Mere Christianity.*

Between his published and broadcasting work, Lewis was becoming well known far beyond the walls of Oxford. Letters poured in from both an admiring and annoyed audience. More opportunities came his way. In June 1941, he delivered a sermon entitled "The Weight of Glory." It would become one his most famous essays when published later.

Another duty Lewis performed was to serve as a Royal Air Force lecturer. Beginning in April 1941, he spent weekends traveling to RAF bases around the country speaking to young soldiers as well as their chaplains. This heightened his awareness of the topics—and spiritual battles—the average person dealt with.

All of these activities occurred while Lewis was still tutoring and lecturing full-time at Magdalen College in Oxford.

The Creation of Screwtape

The seed of the idea that would become *The Screwtape Letters* presented itself to C. S. Lewis in the summer of 1940. Lewis had been ill for several weeks, and as soon as

3. Major Warren "Warnie" Hamilton Lewis (1895–1973) was C. S. Lewis's older brother. Warnie lived with C. S. Lewis throughout most of their adult lives. He was an author, specializing in books about French history. He also compiled the first collection of letters by C. S. Lewis, published in 1966 (*Letters of C. S. Lewis,* London: Geoffrey Bles Ltd.).

he felt able, he returned to his local Anglican church—Holy Trinity, Headington Quarry—for the midday service. Rev. Arthur William Blanchett, the young curate, preached. "But not very favorably," Lewis reported in a letter to his brother, Warnie,[3] in July.

Before the service had ended, Lewis was struck by an idea for a book, an idea that he told Warnie "might be both useful and entertaining." He initially wanted to call it *As One Devil to Another* as it "would consist of letters from an elderly retired devil to a young devil who has just started work on his first 'patient.'" He continued:

> The idea would be to give all the psychology of temptation from the other point of view, e.g., "About undermining his faith in prayer, I don't think you need have any difficulty with his intellect, provided you never say the wrong thing at the wrong moment. After all, the Enemy will either answer his prayers or not. If he does *not,* then that's simple—it shows prayers are no good. If He *does*—I've always found that, oddly enough, this can be just as easily

utilised. It needs only a word from you to make him believe that the very fact of feeling more patient after he's prayed for patience will be taken as proof that prayer is a kind of self-hypnosis. Or if it is answered by some external event, then since that even will have causes which you can point to, he can be persuaded that it would have happened anyway. You see the idea? Prayer can always be discredited either because it works or because it doesn't."[4]

Readers of *The Screwtape Letters* will recognize how Lewis used this idea in "Letter 27." The letter to his brother also serves as a good example of how Lewis's mind was already working through the foundational aspects of what the collection of letters would be.

Lewis was a subscriber to *The Guardian,* a weekly Anglican newspaper (not to be confused with the current British newspaper). In fact, it was the only periodical he received. After completing all thirty-one letters, he offered them to the editor, who had already agreed to publish Lewis's essay "The Dangers of National Repentance."[5]

4. Letter dated July 20–21, 1940, in *Collected Letters II.*

5. "The Dangers of National Repentance" was published in *The Guardian* on March 15, 1940. Within two months, on May 3, another essay—"Two Ways with the Self"—appeared in those pages. Both can be found in Lewis's *God in the Dock.*

A deal was struck, with *The Guardian* offering to pay him two pounds for each letter. (Lewis refused to accept the money, opting instead to have the total dispersed to various widows and orphans, a practice he would continue throughout the rest of his life.)[6] The first letter appeared on May 2, 1941.

The letters were hugely successful, causing even nonsubscribers to seek out *The Guardian* just to read the weekly installments. Watching the success of the letters, publisher Ashley Sampson saw a bestseller in the making. By this time, Centenary Press had been bought by Geoffrey Bles Publishing, and Sampson suggested to the editors that they grab up *The Screwtape Letters* before another publisher beat them to it. They agreed and the book was released in England in February 1942. It appeared in the United States several months later.

Like all his other books, Lewis wrote *Screwtape* in longhand[7] and Warnie typed it into a final draft. Normally Lewis would then burn the original longhand version. But because of the German Blitz on London, Lewis was afraid the original typed manuscript might be destroyed in an air raid. He sent the longhand manuscript for safekeeping to his friend, Sister Penelope, an Anglican nun at the convent of the Community of St. Mary the Virgin at Wantage.[8] After the war, Sister Penelope offered to return the manuscript. Lewis suggested that she sell it, if possible, and put the money to good use. Eventually she sold it to the Berg Collection of the New York Public Library and used the funds to restore the convent's chapel.

Writing *Screwtape,* as Lewis readily admitted, was an unpleasant experience as it forced him to take on the deeply cynical view of a demon who tempts and perverts. It distressed him to write so much, and so easily, from that perspective. Biographer and friend George Sayer surmises in his *Jack:*[9] *C. S. Lewis and His Times* that it may not have been coincidence that around this time Lewis turned to the Cowley Fathers— the Church of England priests of the Society of St. John the Evangelist—for spiritual direction, confession, and advice. This was a practice he continued for many years after *Screwtape* was but a memory.

The Screwtape Letters also utilizes a particular literary approach, uncommon for Lewis at that time, which presents a negative point

8. Wantage is a market town in Oxfordshire (though in 1941 it was in Berkshire), located in southeast England. The convent of the Community of St. Mary the Virgin still exists.

9. Jack was the name C. S. Lewis adopted for himself as a child. It was commonly used by his family and close friends. The British practice at the time, though, was to call men by their last names.

10. Letter dated January 1947, in *Collected Letters II.*

of view to lift up the positive—an approach Lewis suggested would give a fresh, even comical perspective on the subject and attract readers who might not normally think about such things. In 1947, Lewis refused permission for a scholar to create an index for *The Screwtape Letters* because "part of the success of that book depends on luring the ordinary reader into a serious self-knowledge *under pretense* of being a kind of joke." Lewis stated that a subject index would turn the joke into something to be taken seriously. "Of course, this would not deter readers like you," he wrote. "But it is the worldly reader I specially want to catch."[10]

Catching readers—both worldly and otherwise—was something at which C. S. Lewis excelled, as you'll see in these pages.

—Paul McCusker
Colorado Springs
April 2012

Works Cited

Grateful acknowledgment is made to the publishers and copyright holders for permission to reproduce the following material. Because there are so many editions of these titles, I do not provide page numbers but defer to chapters, dates of letters, or other means to source the quotes used.

Allegory of Love.
> C. S. Lewis. *The Allegory of Love: A Study in Medieval Tradition.* Oxford: Clarendon Press, 1936; New York: Oxford Univ. Press, 1960.

Arthurian Torso.
> Charles Williams and C. S. Lewis. *Arthurian Torso, Containing the Posthumous Fragment of the Figure of Arthur by Charles Williams and a Commentary on the Arthurian Poems of Charles Williams by C. S. Lewis.* London: Oxford Univ. Press, 1948.

At Breakfast.
> C. S. Lewis. *C. S. Lewis at the Breakfast Table and Other Reminiscences.* Edited by James T. Como. New York: Macmillan, 1979.

Brothers and Friends.
   W. H. Lewis. *Brothers and Friends: The Diaries of Major Warren Hamilton Lewis.* Edited by Clyde S. Kilby and Marjorie Lamp Mead. San Francisco: HarperCollins, 1982.

Christian Reflections.
   C. S. Lewis. *Christian Reflections.* Edited by Walter Hooper. London: Geoffrey Bles, 1967; Grand Rapids, MI: W. B. Eerdmans, 1967.

Collected Letters II.
   C. S. Lewis. *The Collected Letters of C. S. Lewis, Vol. II: Books, Broadcasts, and the War 1931–1949.* Edited by Walter Hooper. San Francisco: HarperCollins, 2004.

Collected Letters III.
   C. S. Lewis. *The Collected Letters of C. S. Lewis, Vol. III: Narnia, Cambridge, and Joy 1950–1963.* Edited by Walter Hooper. San Francisco: HarperCollins, 2007.

Discarded Image.
   C. S. Lewis. *The Discarded Image: An Introduction to Medieval and Renaissance Literature.* Cambridge Univ. Press, 1964.

English Literature.
   C. S. Lewis. *English Literature in the Sixteenth Century Excluding Drama.* Oxford: Clarendon Press, 1954; New York: Oxford Univ. Press, 1954.

Experiment in Criticism.
C. S. Lewis. *An Experiment in Criticism.*
Cambridge Univ. Press, 1961.

Four Loves.
C. S. Lewis. *The Four Loves.* London: Geoffrey
Bles, 1960; New York: Harcourt, Brace, and
World, 1960.

God in the Dock.
C. S. Lewis. *God in the Dock: Essays on Theology
and Ethics.* Edited by Walter Hooper. Grand
Rapids, MI: W. B. Eerdmans, 1970.

Last Battle.
C. S. Lewis. *The Last Battle.* London: Bodley
Head, 1956.

Letters to an American Lady.
C. S. Lewis. *Letters to an American Lady.*
Edited by Clyde S. Kilby. Grand Rapids, MI:
W. B. Eerdmans, 1967; London: Hodder and
Stoughton, 1969.

Letters to Malcolm.
C. S. Lewis. *Letters to Malcolm, Chiefly on Prayer.*
London: Geoffrey Bles, 1964; New York:
Harcourt, Brace, and World, 1964.

Lewis: A Complete Guide.
C. S. Lewis. *C. S. Lewis: A Complete Guide to
His Life and Works.* Edited by Walter Hooper.
San Francisco: HarperCollins, 1996.

MacDonald: An Anthology.
George MacDonald. *George MacDonald: An Anthology.* Edited by C. S. Lewis. London: Geoffrey Bles, 1946; New York: Macmillan, 1947.

Medieval and Renaissance Literature.
C. S. Lewis. *Studies in Medieval and Renaissance Literature.* Edited by Walter Hooper. Cambridge Univ. Press, 1966.

Mere Christianity.
C. S. Lewis. *Mere Christianity.* London: Geoffrey Bles, 1952; New York: Macmillan, 1952.

Narrative Poems.
C. S. Lewis. *Narrative Poems.* Edited by Walter Hooper. London: Geoffrey Bles, 1969; New York: Harcourt Brace Jovanovich, 1972.

Preface to Paradise Lost.
C. S. Lewis. *A Preface to Paradise Lost.* Oxford Univ. Press, 1942.

Problem of Pain.
C. S. Lewis. *The Problem of Pain.* London: Centenary Press, 1940; New York: Macmillan, 1962.

Reflections on the Psalms.
C. S. Lewis. *Reflections on the Psalms.* London: Geoffrey Bles, 1958; New York: Harcourt, Brace, and World, 1958.

Screwtape Letters.
  C. S. Lewis. *The Screwtape Letters and Screwtape Proposes a Toast.* New York: Macmillan, 1961.

Surprised By Joy.
  C. S. Lewis. *Surprised By Joy: The Shape of My Early Life.* London: Geoffrey Bles, 1955; New York: Harcourt, Brace, and World, 1956.

Surprised By Laughter.
  Terry Lindvall. *Surprised By Laughter: The Comic World of C. S. Lewis.* Nashville: Thomas Nelson, 1996.

Weight of Glory.
  C. S. Lewis. *The Weight of Glory and Other Addresses.* Revised and Expanded Edition. Edited by Walter Hooper. New York: Macmillan, 1980. Five of these essays originally appeared in *Transposition and Other Addresses* by C. S. Lewis (London: Geoffrey Bles, 1949) and *The Weight of Glory and Other Addresses* (New York: Macmillan, 1949).

World's Last Night.
  C. S. Lewis. *The World's Last Night and Other Essays.* New York: Harcourt Brace Jovanovich, 1960.

Preface to the 1961 Edition

It was during the second German War[1] that the letters of Screwtape appeared in the (now extinct) *Guardian*.[2] I hope they did not hasten its death, but they certainly lost it one reader. A country clergyman wrote to the editor, withdrawing his subscription on the ground that "much of the advice given in these letters seemed to him not only erroneous but positively diabolical."

In general, however, they had a reception I had never dreamed of. Reviews were either laudatory[3] or filled with that sort of anger which tells an author that he has hit his target;[4] sales were at first (by my standards) prodigious, and have continued steady.[5]

Of course, sales do not always mean what authors hope. If you gauged the amount of Bible reading in England by the number of Bibles sold, you would go far astray. Sales of *The Screwtape Letters,* in their own little

This preface was originally written by Lewis in 1960 for the 1961 edition of *The Screwtape Letters and Screwtape Proposes a Toast.* The original preface from 1941 follows. Lewis described the two prefaces to his editor this way: "The 1960 Preface is me speaking in my own person and giving literal autobiographical facts. The 1941 one is part of the fantasy or convention which the Letters employ—spoken by the imaginary C. S. L. who has somehow tapped a diabolical correspondence." (*Collected Letters III.*)

1. World War II.

2. *The Guardian* was a Church of England newspaper founded in 1846 by Richard William Church, a member of the Oxford movement and an outspoken High Church Anglican. The movement was also called the Tractarian movement because of the number of published tracts it produced in aid of its cause. The newspaper successfully lasted 105 years, ceasing publication in 1951. It is not to be confused with *The Manchester Guardian*, a mainstream newspaper, which became *The Guardian* in 1959.

3. The reviews were exceptionally enthusiastic. On February 28, 1942, *The Times Literary Supplement* admitted that it could not predict whether or not the book would be "an enduring piece of satirical writing," but that "Mr. Lewis has contrived to say much that a distracted world greatly requires to hear." *The Manchester Guardian* (February 24, 1942) stated that the book was "sparkling yet truly reverent, in fact a perfect joy, and should become a classic." *The Guardian* itself stated on March 13, 1942, that Lewis was as "anxious to unmask" the strategy of the devils against souls "as our intelligence department to detect the designs of Hitler." Leonard Bacon, writing in *The Saturday Review of Literature* (April 17, 1943), announced, "There is a spectacular and satisfactory nova in the bleak sky of satire," and declared the book "admirable, diverting" and a "remarkably original work." (*Lewis: A Complete Guide.*)

4. Writing *Screwtape* may have cost C. S. Lewis more than a few fans. Irish poet Cecil Day Lewis defeated him for Oxford's prestigious Poetry Chair 194 votes to 173. Warnie Lewis expressed astonishment in his diary on February 8, 1951, over the "virulence of anti-Christian feeling" in the vote. Their good friend Hugo Dyson told Warnie "one elector whom he canvassed announced his intention of voting for C. Day Lewis *on the ground that* Jack had written *Screwtape!*" (*Brothers and Friends.*)

5. Geoffrey Bles released *The Screwtape Letters* in February 1942 with an initial printing of two thousand copies. They

way, suffer from a similar ambiguity. It is the sort of book that gets given to godchildren, the sort that gets read aloud at retreats. It is even, as I have noticed with a chastened smile, the sort that gravitates towards spare bedrooms, there to live a life of undisturbed tranquility in company with[6] *The Roadmender,*[7] *John Inglesant,*[8] and *The Life of the Bee.*[9] Sometimes it is bought for even more humiliating reasons. A lady whom I knew discovered that the pretty little probationer[10] who filled her hot-water bottle in the hospital had read *Screwtape.* She also discovered why. "You see," said the girl, "we were warned that at interviews, after the real, technical questions are over, matrons and people sometimes ask about your general interests. The best thing is to say you've read something. So they gave us a list of about ten books that usually go down pretty well and said we ought to read at least one of them." "And you chose Screwtape?" "Well, of course; it was the shortest."

Still, when all allowances have been made, the book has had readers of the genuine sort sufficiently numerous to make it worthwhile answering some of the questions it has raised in their minds.

sold out immediately. It was reprinted eight more times before the end of that year. Macmillan and Company released the book in America in 1943. It became an instant bestseller. On September 8, 1947, *Time Magazine* put a painting of Lewis on its cover, with an angel's wing adorning one side and a pitchfork-carrying devil adorning the other.

6. Presumably Lewis chose the three referenced books because many of *The Guardian*'s readers owned them, but he never read them more than once, if at all. His assumption proved to be right in the long run. Few people know the books now.

7. *The Roadmender,* first published in England in 1903, was a collection of reflective essays about the English countryside and explored themes surrounding being disenfranchised from the "road of life." It became hugely popular and had sold 250,000 copies by 1922. The author proved to be a mystery, though, as few could figure out who Michael Fairless was. It was later discovered that Michael Fairless was actually Margaret Fairless Barber (1869–1901), a woman with a spinal condition that ultimately left her an invalid. She wrote the book in the last twenty months of her life.

8. *John Inglesant* was written by Joseph Henry Shorthouse (1834–1903) and published in 1881. The novel chronicles the life and travails of a young man caught up in the political and religious upheaval of seventeenth-century England. For all of its action, it is primarily a didactic work of fic-

tion that explores many of the theological arguments of the time.

9. *The Life of the Bee* (*La Vie des Abeilles*) by French author Maurice Maeterlinck (1862–1949) is a fanciful and lively chronicle of twenty years of beekeeping. It was translated into English and published in 1901.

10. Probationer: a student nurse undergoing a trial period of employment.

11. In *A Preface to Paradise Lost* C. S. Lewis notes that Satan's "revolt is entangled in contradictions from the very outset.... He wants hierarchy and does not want hierarchy. Throughout the poem he is engaged in sawing off the branch he is sitting on, not only in the quasi-political sense already indicated, but in a deeper sense still, since a creature revolting against a creator is revolting against the source of his own powers—including even his power to revolt.... He has become more a Lie than a Liar, a personified self-contradiction.... This doom he has brought upon himself; in order to avoid seeing one thing he has, almost voluntarily, incapacitated himself from seeing at all." (*Preface to Paradise Lost.*)

12. Michael, a name meaning "who is like God," is described as an archangel in Jewish, Christian, and Islamic teaching. He is mentioned in the Book of Daniel, chapter 10, and the Revelation of John, chapter 12.

13. In 1944, C. S. Lewis made a similar statement in his "Answers to Questions on Christianity": "No reference to the Devil or devils is included in any Christian Creeds, and it is quite possible to be a Christian without believing in them. I do believe such beings exist, but that is my own affair. Supposing there to be such beings, the degree to which humans were conscious of their presence would presumably vary very much. I mean, the more a man was in the Devil's power, the less he would be aware of it, on the principle that a man is still fairly sober as long as he knows he's drunk." (*God in the Dock.*)

The commonest question is whether I really "believe in the Devil."

Now, if by "the Devil" you mean a power opposite to God and, like God, self-existent from all eternity, the answer is certainly No. There is no uncreated being except God. God has no opposite. No being could attain a "perfect badness" opposite to the perfect goodness of God; for when you have taken away every kind of good thing (intelligence, will, memory, energy, and existence itself) there would be none of him left.

The proper question is whether I believe in devils. I do. That is to say, I believe in angels, and I believe that some of these, by the abuse of their free will, have become enemies to God and, as a corollary, to us. These we may call devils. They do not differ in nature from good angels, but their nature is depraved. *Devil* is the opposite of *angel* only as Bad Man is the opposite of Good Man. Satan, the leader or dictator of devils,[11] is the opposite, not of God, but of Michael.[12]

I believe this not in the sense that it is part of my creed, but in the sense that it is one of my opinions.[13] My religion would not be in ruins if this opinion were shown to be false. Till that happens—and proofs of a negative are hard to come by—I shall retain it. It seems to me to explain a good many facts. It agrees with the plain sense of Scripture, the tradition of Christendom, and the beliefs of most men at most times. And it conflicts with nothing that any of the sciences has shown to be true.

It should be (but it is not) unnecessary to add that a belief in angels, whether good or evil, does not mean a belief in either as they are represented in art and literature.[14] Devils are depicted with bats' wings and good angels with birds' wings, not because anyone holds that moral deterioration would be likely to turn feathers into membrane, but because most men like birds better than bats. They are given wings at all in order to suggest the swiftness of unimpeded intellectual energy. They are given human form because man is the only rational creature we know. Creatures higher in the natural order than ourselves, either incorporeal or animating bodies of a sort we cannot experience, must be represented symbolically if they are to be represented at all.[15]

These forms are not only symbolical but were always known to be symbolized

14. See how Screwtape expands on this idea in "Letter 7" (p. 39).

15. In the three books comprising his Space Trilogy, Lewis does not follow his own rule about depicting angels. See the "Eldila" in *Out of the Silent Planet*, *Perelandra*, and *That Hideous Strength*, which he created to "smash the nineteenth century *female* angel." (Letter dated March 4, 1953, in *Letters to an American Lady*.)

16. There is some debate about who this Dionysius actually was. Scholar Devin Brown has observed to this author that "Lewis may be referring to the figure now called Pseudo-Dionysius, a Christian theologian of the late fifth and early sixth centuries, and to his work *Celestial Hierarchy*. There Pseudo-Dionysius writes '. . . the prophet described the feel of the Celestial Intelligences as being covered by their wings which symbolize a swift soaring to the heights'. Lewis comments further on the angelic representation according to Pseudo-Dionysius in *The Discarded Image* (chap. 4)."

17. Born Guido di Pietro, Fra Angelico (1395–1455) was an early Italian Renaissance painter as well as a Dominican monk. Some of his most famous paintings depict the Annunciation (Gabriel's appearance to Mary, the mother of Jesus).

18. Raphael Sanzio (1483–1520) was an Italian painter of the High Renaissance. His most famous angels, found at the bottom of *Sistine Madonna,* depict two chubby and infantile beings, which now adorn stamps, postcards, and wrapping paper.

19. Houris are beautiful maidens. Lewis is referencing the Muslim belief that faithful men will be rewarded with beautiful maidens in paradise.

20. "I believe no angel ever appears in Scripture without exciting terror: they always have to begin by saying 'Fear not.'" (Letter dated March 4, 1953, in *Letters to an American Lady.*) See the Gospel of Luke, chapters 1 and 2, for the encounters of

by reflective people. The Greeks did not believe that the gods were really like the beautiful human shapes their sculptors gave them. In their poetry a god who wishes to "appear" to a mortal temporarily assumes the likeness of a man. Christian theology has nearly always explained the "appearance" of an angel in the same way. It is only the ignorant, says Dionysius[16] in the fifth century, who dream that spirits are really winged men.

In the plastic arts these symbols have steadily degenerated. Fra Angelico's[17] angels carry in their face and gesture the peace and authority of heaven. Later come the chubby infantile nudes of Raphael;[18] finally the soft, slim, girlish and consolatory angels of nineteenth-century art, shapes so feminine that they avoid being voluptuous only by their total insipidity—the frigid houris[19] of a tea-table paradise. They are a pernicious symbol. In Scripture the visitation of an angel is always alarming; it has to begin by saying "Fear not."[20] The Victorian angel looks as if it were going to say "There, there."

The literary symbols are more dangerous because they are not so easily recognized as symbolical. Those of Dante[21] are the best. Before his angels we sing in awe. His devils, as Ruskin[22] rightly remarked, in their rage, spite, and obscenity, are far more like what the reality must be than anything in Milton.[23] Milton's devils,[24] by their grandeur and high poetry, have done great harm, and his angels owe too much to Homer[25] and Raphael.[26] But the really pernicious image is Goethe's[27] Mephistopheles. It is Faust, not he, who really exhibits the ruthless, sleepless, unsmiling concentration upon self which is the mark of Hell. The humorous, civilised, sensible, adaptable Mephistopheles has helped to strengthen the illusion that evil is liberating.

A little man may sometimes avoid some single error made by a great one, and I was determined that my own symbolism should at least not err in Goethe's way. For humor involves a sense of proportion and a power of seeing yourself from the outside.[28] Whatever else we attribute to beings who sinned through pride, we must not attribute this. Satan, said Chesterton,[29] fell through force of gravity. We must picture Hell as a state where everyone is perpetually concerned about his own dignity and advancement,

Zechariah, Mary, and a group of shepherds with various angelic appearances. Lewis also depicts a terrifying encounter with an angel in the first two chapters of *Perelandra*.

21. Dante Alighieri (1265–1321) was an Italian poet, moral philosopher, literary theorist, and political thinker. He is best known, and often referred to by Lewis, for his epic work *The Divine Comedy*, which explores a soul's search for God through an afterlife journey to hell, purgatory, and heaven.

22. John Ruskin (1819–1900) was an author, artist, and the leading English art critic of his time. In volume 3, chapter 7, of his *The Stones of Venice*, he explores how demons are portrayed in literature and concludes that "even in the most serious subjects, the fiends are oftener ludicrous than terrible." In comparing John Milton (see note 22) and Dante, he determines that Dante has "deeper insight into the nature of sin. Milton makes his fiends too noble and misses the foulness, inconstancy, and fury of wickedness. His Satan possesses some virtues . . . as opposed to the 'Insania' of excessive sin." Dante, on the other hand, created a "peculiar grandeur in the indescribable, ungovernable fury of Dante's fiends, ever shortening its own powers and disappointing its own purposes; the deaf, blind, speechless, unspeakable rage, fierce as the lightning, but erring from its mark or turning senselessly against itself, and still further debased by foulness of form and action."

23. John Milton (1608–1674) was an English poet, scholar, theologian, and pamphleteer. His epic work *Paradise Lost* is considered one of the greatest poems of English literature.

24. See Lewis's *A Preface to Paradise Lost* (Oxford Univ. Press, 1942), specifically chapter 13 about Satan and chapter 14 where he explores Satan's followers.

25. Homer is the ninth-century Greek poet credited with having written, or at the very least compiled, *The Iliad* and *The Odyssey*.

26. In chapter 3 of *The Discarded Image,* Lewis remarked on Dante's "individual genius" behind the "unrivalled majesty" of his angels. On Milton, he determined that he "missed the target." Milton's "angels have too much anatomy and too much armour, are too much like the gods of Homer and Virgil. . . . After Milton total degradation sets in and we finally reach the purely consolatory, hence waterishly feminine, angels of nineteenth-century art."

27. Johann Wolfgang von Goethe (1749–1832) was a German poet, dramatist, and novelist. His dramatic poem *Faust* chronicled the German legend of a man who sells his soul to Mephistopheles, the devil, to gain vast knowledge and worldly pleasure. Lewis expounds upon Goethe's work in chapter 10 of the novel *Perelandra* (London: John Lane, 1943).

28. For Screwtape's twisted perspective on humor, see "Letter 11" (p. 63).

29. A quote from chapter 8 of G. K. Chesterton's *Orthodoxy* (New York: John Lane, 1908). Gilbert Keith Chesterton (1874–1936) was a prolific English writer whose works included essays, novels, plays, poetry, biographies, and literary and art reviews. He may be known best for his Father Brown mysteries. Lewis was deeply affected by his works of Christian apologetics, especially *The Everlasting Man*. In 1962, Lewis included it in his list of the ten books that influenced him the most (see the appendix on page 219 for the complete list).

where everyone has a grievance, and where everyone lives the deadly serious passions of envy, self-importance, and resentment.[30] This, to begin with. For the rest, my own choice of symbols depended, I suppose, on temperament and on the age.

I like bats much better than bureaucrats. I live in the Managerial Age,[31] in a world of "Admin." The greatest evil is not now done in those sordid "dens of crime" that Dickens[32] loved to paint. It is not done even in concentration camps and labour camps. In those we see its final result. But it is conceived and ordered (moved, seconded, carried, and minuted) in clean, carpeted, warmed, and well-lighted offices, by quiet men with white collars and cut fingernails and smooth-shaven cheeks who do not need to raise their voice.[33] Hence, naturally enough, my symbol for Hell is something like the bureaucracy of a police state or the offices of a thoroughly nasty business concern.

Milton has told us that "devil with devil damned Firm concord holds."[34] But how? Certainly not by friendship. A being which can still love is not yet a devil. Here again my symbol seemed to me useful. It enabled

30. In chapter 13 of *A Preface to Paradise Lost,* Lewis states about Satan: "In the midst of a world of light and love, of song and feast and dance, he could find nothing to think of than his own prestige."

31. Possibly a reference to the 1941 book *The Managerial Revolution* by American philosopher James Burnham (1905–1987), which espoused the view that managers were the "ruling class of the new society."

32. Charles Dickens (1812–1870), an English novelist, wrote dozens of classics during the Victorian era, including *Oliver Twist, David Copperfield,* and *A Christmas Carol.* "Dens of crime" were especially described in *Oliver Twist.*

33. Lewis depicts this world more fully through the operations of N.I.C.E. (National Institute of Coordinated Experiments) in *That Hideous Strength* (London: Bodley Head, 1945).

34. From John Milton's *Paradise Lost,* book 2.

The court of Miraz in *Prince Caspian* (London: Geoffrey Bles, 1951) represents this reality. Miraz has killed his brother and stolen the crown. He is determined to destroy Caspian, the rightful heir. He is ultimately betrayed and murdered by two lords, Glozelle and Sopespian.

me, by earthly parallels, to picture an official society held together entirely by fear and greed. On the surface, manners are normally suave. Rudeness to one's superiors would obviously be suicidal; rudeness to one's equals might put them on their guard before you were ready to spring your mine. For of course "Dog eat dog" is the principle of the whole organisation. Everyone wishes everyone else's discrediting, demotion, and ruin; everyone is an expert in the confidential report, the pretended alliance, the stab in the back. Over all this their good manners, their expressions of grave respect, their "tributes" to one another's invaluable services form a thin crust. Every now and then it gets punctured, and the scalding lava of their hatred spurts out.[35]

This symbol also enabled me to get rid of the absurd fancy that devils are engaged in the disinterested pursuit of something called Evil (the capital is essential). Mine have no use for any such turnip ghost. Bad angels, like bad men, are entirely practical. They have two motives. The first is fear of punishment: for as totalitarian countries have their camps for torture, so my Hell contains deeper Hells, its "houses of correction."

Their second motive is a kind of hunger. I feign that devils can, in a spiritual sense, eat one another; and us. Even in human life we have seen the passion to dominate, almost to digest, one's fellow; to make his whole intellectual and emotional life merely an extension of one's own—to hate one's hatreds and resent one's grievances and indulge one's egoism through him as well as through oneself. His own little store of passion must of course be suppressed to make room for ours. If he resists this suppression he is being very selfish.

On Earth this desire is often called "love." In Hell I feign that they recognize it as hunger. But there the hunger is more ravenous, and a fuller satisfaction is possible. There, I suggest, the stronger spirit—there are perhaps no bodies to impede the operation—can really and irrevocably suck the weaker into itself and permanently gorge its own being on the weaker's outraged individuality.[36] It is (I feign) for this that devils desire human souls and the souls of one another. It is for this that Satan desires all his own followers and all the sons of Eve and all the host of Heaven. His dream is of the day when all shall be inside him

36. Lewis demonstrates this at the beginning of "Letter 31" (p. 183).

37. See "Letter 8" (p. 45) for more on this idea.

38. *Des träumte mir nur* means "I only dreamed of," the statement of the bride-to-be in a tale by Jacob Grimm (1785–1863) and Wilhelm Grimm (1786–1859), German academics who collected legends and folklore into their now famous *Grimm's Fairy Tales*. Lewis is referring to "The Robber Bridegroom," in which a young girl is betrothed to a murderer and, after visiting his house, witnessing a terrible murder, and narrowly escaping with the help of an old woman, tells the tale of her visit on their wedding day. The Robber Bridegroom repeatedly calls her tale "only a dream," whereupon the girl presents gruesome evidence and her murderous bridegroom is captured.

39. There is speculation by some scholars that Lewis is referring to *Infernal Conference, or Dialogues of Devils* written in 1772 by Baptist minister John Macgowan and published under the pseudonym The Listener. In this lineage of diabolical writings can also be found *Letters from Hell* by the Danish priest and author Valdemar Adolph Thisted (1815–1887), which Lewis *did* read and disliked. That book came to Lewis's attention via George MacDonald, a pastor, fantasy writer, and influence on Lewis, who had written the preface to an 1884 edition of Thisted's book. It has also been noted that Thisted's book includes the arrival in hell of the narrator's mother, drawing comparisons to the mother described in *The Screwtape Letters*. For more on this, see Douglas A. Anderson's *Tales*

and all that says "I" can say it only through him. This, I surmise, is the bloated-spider parody, the only imitation he can understand, of that unfathomed bounty whereby God turns tools into servants and servants into sons, so that they may be at last reunited to Him in the perfect freedom of a love offered from the height of the utter individualities which he has liberated them to be.[37]

But, as in Grimm's story, *des träumte mir nur*,[38] this is all only myth and symbol. That is why the question of my own opinion about devils, though proper to be answered when once it was raised, is really of very minor importance for a reader of *Screwtape*. To those who share that opinion, my devils will be symbols of a concrete reality: to others, they will be personifications of abstractions, and the book will be an allegory. But it makes little difference which way you read it. For of course its purpose was not to speculate about diabolical life but to throw light from a new angle on the life of men.

I am told that I was not first in the field and that someone in the seventeenth century wrote letters from a devil.[39] I have not seen that book. I believe its slant was mainly political. But I gladly acknowledge a debt to Stephen McKenna *The Confessions of a Well-Meaning Woman*.[40] The connection may not be obvious, but you will find there the same moral inversion—the blacks all white and the whites all black—and the humour which comes of speaking through a totally humourless *personna*. I think my idea of spiritual cannibalism probably owes something to the horrible scenes of "absorbing" in David Lindsay's neglected [*A*] *Voyage to Arcturus*.[41]

The names of my devils have excited a good deal of curiosity, and there have been many explanations, all wrong. The truth is that I aimed merely at making them nasty—and here too I am perhaps indebted to Lindsay—by the sound. Once a name was invented, I might speculate like anyone else (and with no more authority than anyone else) as to the phonetic associations, which caused the unpleasant effect. I fancy that *Scrooge, screw, thumbscrew, tapeworm,* and *red tape* all do some work in my hero's name, and that *slob, slobber, slubber,* and *gob* have all gone into *slubgob*.

Some have paid me an undeserved compliment by supposing that my *Letters* were

Before Narnia: The Roots of Modern Fantasy and Science Fiction (New York: Del Ray Books, 2008).

40. Stephen McKenna (1888–1967) was a British-born and Oxford-educated writer whose works included *The Reluctant Lover* (1912), *Sonia* (1917), *The Education of Eric Lane* (1921), and *The Magic Quest* (1933). He also traveled extensively during the 1920s and 1930s, his journeys taking him to South America, the Caribbean, and Africa. Written in 1922, *The Confessions of a Well-Meaning Woman* was a critically applauded satire of the British upper class and reflected McKenna's own experiences in that social world.

41. David Lindsay (1876–1945) was an author of Scottish descent who wrote science fiction that explored philosophical, theological, and metaphysical ideas. Though he had little financial success, his works influenced both C. S. Lewis and J. R. R. Tolkien. His *A Voyage to Arcturus,* published in 1920, was a unique blending of fantasy, science fiction, philosophy, and theology. The story chronicled an intergalactic voyage between star systems and planets, each representative of states of the mind. Friend Arthur Greeves first suggested the book to C. S. Lewis in 1934. In a letter dated October 29, 1944, Lewis credited this book for giving him the idea that the two elements of science fiction and the supernatural could be effectively combined. (*Collected Letters II.*)

42. Psalm 36:1, as rendered in the Book of Common Prayer. See also chapter 12 of Lewis's *Reflections on the Psalms.*

43. A reference to *Gulliver's Travels,* a satirical novel by Jonathan Swift (1667–1745) in which Gulliver is, in one adventure, a giant in a land of little people and, later, a tiny man in a land of giants.

44. *Erewhon, or Over the Range* by Samuel Butler (1835–1902) was a satire of utopian ideals where crimes are handled through hospital treatment or surgically. Butler is best known for his semiautobiographical *The Way of All Flesh* and his translations of Homer's *The Iliad* and *The Odyssey.*

45. F. Anstey was the pseudonym of British author Thomas Anstey Guthrie (1856–1934). The Garuda Stone appeared in his novel *Vice Versa,* in which a father and son are magically switched by the stone into each other's bodies and lives. This idea has been used in many stories and films, often without credit to the author.

the ripe fruit of many years' study in moral and ascetic theology. They forgot that there is an equally reliable, though less creditable, way of learning how temptation works. "My heart"—I need no other's—"showeth me the wickedness of the ungodly."[42]

I was often asked or advised to add to the original *Letters,* but for many years I felt not the least inclination to do it. Though I had never written anything more easily, I never wrote with less enjoyment. The ease came, no doubt, from the fact that the device of diabolical letters, once you have thought of it, exploits itself spontaneously, like Swift's big and little men,[43] or the medical and ethical philosophy of *Erewhon,*[44] or Anstey's Garuda Stone.[45] It would run away with you for a thousand pages if you gave it its head. But though it was easy to twist one's mind into the diabolical attitude, it was not fun, or not for long. The strain produced a sort of spiritual cramp. The work into which I had to project myself while I spoke through Screwtape was all dust, grit, thirst, and itch. Every trace of beauty, freshness, and geniality had to be excluded. It almost smothered me before I was done. It would have smothered my readers if I had prolonged it.

I had, moreover, a sort of grudge against my book for not being a different book which no one could write. Ideally, Screwtape's advice to Wormwood should have been balanced by arch-angelical advice to the patient's guardian angel.[46] Without this the picture of human life is lopsided. But who could supply the deficiency? Even if a man—and he would have to be a far better man than I—could scale the spiritual heights required, what "answerable style"[47] could he use? For the style would really be part of the content. Mere advice would be no good; every sentence would have to smell of Heaven. And nowadays even if you could write a prose like Traherne's,[48] you wouldn't be allowed to, for the canon of "functionalism"[49] has disabled literature for half its functions. (At bottom, every ideal of style dictates not only how we should say things but what sort of things we may say.)

Then, as years went on and the stifling experience of writing the *Letters* became a weaker memory, reflections on this and that which seemed somehow to demand Screwtapian treatment began to occur to me. I was resolved never to write another *Letter*. The idea of something like a lecture

46. As it is, there are hints of the patient's guardian angels throughout the book, and those angels are referenced in the final paragraph of "Letter 31" (p. 183).

47. A reference to Milton's *Paradise Lost*, book 9, in which Milton struggles with the difficulty of the story he must tell about "the Fall of Man," but hopes to balance it with an "answerable style I can obtain of my celestial patroness." Lewis makes an attempt at the speech of archangels in the long prose poem of the Great Dance in chapter 17 of *Perelandra* (London: John Lane, 1943).

48. Thomas Traherne (1636?–1674) was an English poet and author of religious essays. Lewis considered Traherne's *Centuries of Meditations* "almost the most beautiful book (in prose, I mean, excluding poets) in English." (Letter to Arthur Greeves, December 23, 1941, in *Collected Letters II*.)

49. Functionalism sought to dissect, explain, and categorize literary expression, creating a rigid school of criticism regarding how to approach subject matter and style, which Lewis obviously did not appreciate.

50. *The Saturday Evening Post* was an American weekly magazine published between 1897 and 1969. (It would later be offered as a bimonthly publication.) *Screwtape Proposes a Toast* appeared in the magazine on December 19, 1959.

51. C. S. Lewis is often associated with Magdalen (pronounced "Maudlin") College, Oxford, having tutored there from 1924 until he began teaching at Magdalene College, Cambridge, in 1954. *The Screwtape Letters* and its original preface, then, were written while Lewis taught at Oxford. *Screwtape Proposes a Toast* and its preface were written after he had become a professor at Cambridge. On November 29, 1954, Lewis gave his inaugural lecture at Cambridge, in which he famously described himself as a "dinosaur." It was his birthday on the day of the lecture. He was all of fifty-six years old.

or "address" hovered vaguely in my mind, now forgotten, now recalled, never written. Then came an invitation from *The Saturday Evening Post*,[50] and that pressed the trigger.

—C. S. Lewis
Magdalene College,
Cambridge[51]
18th May 1960

The best way to drive out the devil, if he will not yield to texts of scripture, is to jeer and flout him, for he cannot bear scorn.

—*Martin Luther*

The devill . . . the Prowde spirite . . . cannot endure to be mocked.

—*Thomas More*

Martin Luther (1483–1546) was a priest, academic, author, and ultimately the founder of the German Reformation. This quote comes from "Of the Devil and His Works," chapter 25 of Luther's *Table Talk*. First published by Johannes Aurifaber in 1566, this is the earliest known rendering of the quote, which is part of a much longer section about chasing the devil away by using scorn. English adventurer Captain Henry Bell translated sections of *Table Talk* into English in 1650. In the early nineteenth century, the quote was referenced by Scottish biographer Alexander Chalmers (1759–1834) in his memoir of Luther and used as part of *The Table Talk of Martin Luther* as translated by English writer William Hazlitt (1778–1830). Lewis was certainly familiar with the works of Hazlitt and may have picked up the quote from him.

Thomas More (1478–1535) was the lord chancellor of England from 1529 to 1532, until he had to resign over his opposition to King Henry VIII's divorce. He was eventually beheaded for defying the king's Act of Succession and Act of Supremacy. This quote comes from book 2, chapter 16, of his *A Dialogue of Comfort Against Tribulation,* in which advice is given about how to get rid of the devil's temptations: "Some folk have been clearly rid of such pestilent phantasies with very full contempt thereof, making a cross upon their hearts and bidding the devil avaunt, and sometime laugh him to scorn, too, and then turn their mind unto some other matter. And when the devil hath seen that they have set so little by him, after many essays, made in such times as he thought most meet, he hath given that temptation quite over, both for that the proud spirit cannot endure to be mocked."

Preface to the Original Edition

I have no intention of explaining how the correspondence which I now offer to the public fell into my hands.

There are two equal and opposite errors into which our race can fall about the devils. One is to disbelieve in their existence. The other is to believe, and to feel an excessive and unhealthy interest in them.[1] They themselves are equally pleased by both errors and hail a materialist or a magician with the same delight. The sort of script which is used in this book can be very easily obtained by anyone who has once learned the knack; but ill disposed or excitable people who might make a bad use of it shall not learn it from me.

Readers are advised to remember that the devil is a liar. Not everything that Screwtape says should be assumed to be true even from his own angle. I have made no attempt to identify any of the human

1. In chapter 4 of *Surprised By Joy*, Lewis relates how he fell into this category as a young man under the guidance of Miss Cowie, the matron at his school. His interest in the occult would stay with him his entire life.

2. During World War II, Britain introduced rationing policies to govern the distribution of food, petrol, and other everyday items. Rationing did not officially end in that country until 1954.

3. This is not the only instance in his books when Lewis allowed for alternate realities of time. Throughout *The Chronicles of Narnia,* the characters from our world experienced a distortion of time, as they understood it. The four Pevensie children reached adulthood in Narnia, in *The Lion, the Witch, and the Wardrobe,* only to return to our world mere minutes after they'd left it.

4. World War II, which began on September 1, 1939.

5. Magdalen College, founded in 1458, is one of thirty-eight colleges on the Oxford University campus. C. S. Lewis was elected a fellow (a scholar appointed by a university to reside and work at one of its colleges) of Magdalen College on May 20, 1925. He served there as a tutor in English language and literature until 1954.

beings mentioned in the letters; but I think it very unlikely that the portraits, say, of Fr. Spike or the patient's mother, are wholly just. There is wishful thinking in Hell as well as on Earth.

In conclusion, I ought to add that no effort has been made to clear up the chronology of the letters. Number XVII appears to have been composed before rationing[2] became serious; but in general the diabolical method of dating seems to bear no relation to terrestrial time[3] and I have not attempted to reproduce it. The history of the European War,[4] except in so far as it happens now and then to impinge upon the spiritual condition of one human being, was obviously of no interest to Screwtape.

—C. S. Lewis
Magdalen College[5]
5 July 1941

The
Screwtape
Letters

Letter 1

My dear Wormwood,[1]

 note what you say about guiding your patient's reading[2] and taking care that he sees a good deal of his materialist friend. But are you not being a trifle *naif*? It sounds as if you supposed that *argument* was the way to keep him out of the Enemy's clutches.[3] That might have been so if he had lived a few centuries earlier. At that time the humans still knew pretty well when a thing was proved and when it was not; and if it was proved they really believed it. They still connected thinking with doing and were prepared to alter their way of life as the result of a chain of reasoning. But what with the weekly press and other such weapons we have largely altered that. Your man has been accustomed, ever since he was a boy, to have a dozen

This first letter was published in *The Guardian* on May 2, 1941.

1. From the Old English *wormod* (or *wermod*), a woody shrub (*Artemisia*), which has a bitter aromatic taste. It is used in the preparation of vermouth and absinthe and some medicines. C. S. Lewis wrote a poem called "Wormwood" included in *The Pilgrim's Regress*. An excerpt:
> "Thou only art alternative to God, oh, dark
> And burning island among spirit, tenth
>   hierarch,
> Wormwood, immortal Satan, Ahriman,
>   alone
> Second to Him to whom no second else
>   were known . . ."
> —Lewis, *The Pilgrim's Regress*, bk. 10, chap. 1 (London: J. M. Dent and Sons, 1933).

2. Lewis notes in *Surprised By Joy* that "a young man who wishes to remain a sound atheist cannot be too careful of his reading." It was through friendship and reading that Lewis became a Christian.

3. In a letter to his brother, Warnie, dated July 19, 1940, Lewis described some of his early concepts for what would become *The Screwtape Letters*. Lewis wrote as the demon: "In attacking the faith, I should be chary of argument. Arguments only provoke answers. What you want to work away at is the mere unreasonable *feeling* that 'that sort of thing can't really be true.'" (*Collected Letters II.*)

4. This subject comes up again in "Letter 27" (p. 159) as the Historical Point of View. Lewis discusses his own "chronological snobbery" in chapter 13 of *Surprised By Joy.*

incompatible philosophies dancing about together inside his head. He doesn't think of doctrines as primarily "true" or "false," but as "academic" or "practical," "outworn" or "contemporary," "conventional" or "ruthless." Jargon, not argument, is your best ally in keeping him from the Church. Don't waste time trying to make him think that materialism is *true*! Make him think it is strong, or stark, or courageous—that it is the philosophy of the future.[4] That's the sort of thing he cares about.

The trouble about argument is that it moves the whole struggle onto the Enemy's own ground. He can argue too; whereas in really practical propaganda of the kind I am suggesting He has been shown for centuries to be greatly the inferior of Our Father Below. By the very act of arguing, you awake the patient's reason; and once it is awake, who can foresee the result? Even if a particular train of thought can be twisted so as to end in our favour, you will find that you have been strengthening in your patient the fatal habit of attending to universal issues and withdrawing his attention from the stream of immediate sense experiences. Your business is to fix his attention on the stream. Teach him to call it "real life" and don't let him ask what he means by "real."

Remember, he is not, like you, a pure spirit. Never having been a human (Oh that abominable advantage of the Enemy's!) you don't realize how enslaved they are to the pressure of the ordinary. I once had a patient, a sound atheist, who used to read in the British Museum.[5] One day, as he sat reading, I saw a train of thought in his mind beginning to go the wrong way. The Enemy, of course, was at his elbow in a moment. Before I knew where I was I saw my twenty years' work beginning to totter. If I had lost my head and begun to attempt a defence by argument I should have been undone. But I was not such a fool. I struck instantly at the part of the man which I had best under my control and suggested that it was just about time he had some lunch. The Enemy presumably made the counter-suggestion (you know how one can never *quite* overhear what He says to them?) that this was more important than lunch. At least I think that must have been His line for when I said, "Quite. In fact much too important to tackle at the end of a morning," the patient brightened up considerably;

5. Established in 1753, the British Museum contained one of the largest and most comprehensive collections of books, artifacts, galleries, and treasures found in the world. The Reading Room, built in 1857, stood at the center of the museum and was frequented by both casual readers and researchers. In 1997, it was replaced by the current British Library.

6. Many correspondents at the time noted to Lewis that the "patient" could not have seen the number 73 bus from anywhere near the British Museum. Lewis wrestled with the correction in 1960 while preparing the manuscript for the combined book of *The Screwtape Letters and Screwtape Proposes a Toast.* On October 9, 1960, he wrote to Jocelyn Gibb, his editor at Geoffrey Bles, that the bus "need not be visible *from* the [British Museum]." He conceded that he was prepared to change the bus number, or even change the vehicle from a bus to a "green coach, jeep, fire engine, Rolls, police car, or ambulance" if a solution couldn't be sorted out. "Take your choice," he wrote. In the end, he changed the original wording from "street" to "streets" and from "before he had reached the bottom of the steps" to "before he had gone very far." On October 12, Lewis wrote to Gibb, "I do believe we've got it right at last." (*Collected Letters III.*)

and by the time I had added, "Much better come back after lunch and go into it with a fresh mind," he was already halfway to the door. Once he was in the streets the battle was won. I showed him a newsboy shouting the midday paper, and a No. 73[6] bus going past, and before he had gone very far I had got into him an unalterable conviction that, whatever odd ideas might come into a man's head when he was shut up alone with his books, a healthy dose of "real life" (by which he meant the bus and the newsboy) was enough to show him that all "that sort of thing" just couldn't be true. He knew he'd had a narrow escape and in later years was fond of talking about "that inarticulate sense for actuality which is our ultimate safeguard against the aberrations of mere logic." He is now safe in Our Father's house.

You begin to see the point? Thanks to processes which we set at work in them centuries ago, they find it all but impossible to believe in the unfamiliar while the familiar is before their eyes. Keep pressing home on him the *ordinariness* of things. Above all, do not attempt to use science (I mean, the real sciences) as a defence against

Christianity. They will positively encourage him to think about realities he can't touch and see. There have been sad cases among the modern physicists. If he must dabble in science, keep him on economics. And sociology; don't let him get away from that invaluable "real life." But the best of all is to let him read no science but to give him a grand general idea that he knows it all and that everything he happens to have picked up in casual talk and reading is "the results of modern investigation." Do remember you are there to fuddle him. From the way some of you young fiends talk, anyone would suppose it was our job to teach!

Your affectionate uncle
Screwtape

Letter 2

My dear Wormwood,

First published in *The Guardian* on May 9, 1941.

I note with grave displeasure that your patient has become a Christian. Do not indulge the hope that you will escape the usual penalties; indeed, in your better moments, I trust you would hardly even wish to do so. In the meantime we must make the best of the situation. There is no need to despair; hundreds of these adult converts have been reclaimed after a brief sojourn in the Enemy's camp and are now with us. All the *habits* of the patient, both mental and bodily, are still in our favour.

One of our great allies at present is the Church itself. Do not misunderstand me. I do not mean the Church as we see her spread out through all time and space and rooted in eternity, terrible as an army with banners. That, I confess, is a spectacle

1. A "building estate" is a planned community, with homes designed after a handful of basic models, a shopping area, a pub or two, and of course a church, more than likely belonging to the Church of England.

2. Readers at the time this was written would recognize the "shiny little book" to be *The Book of Common Prayer and Administration of the Sacraments and Other Rites and Ceremonies of the Church According to the Use of the Church of England: Together with the Psalter or Psalms of David Pointed as They Are To Be Sung or Said in Churches and the Form or Manner of Making Ordaining and Consecrating of Bishops Priests and Deacons.* Originally compiled by Archbishop of Canterbury Thomas Cranmer in 1549, with revisions in 1552 and the "final" version in 1662, it incorporated the established liturgy and rites for the Church of England services. Not surprisingly, by 1941 the language and forms of worship may have seemed archaic and outdated to some.

3. The "shabby little book" would have been a hymnal or, more specifically, an edition of *Hymns Ancient and Modern for Use in the Services of the Church* produced by the Church of England.

4. "The Body of Christ" references the Anglican understanding of believers in Christ as members of Christ's "body" on earth (or "the church"). This concept can be found throughout the New Testament in the Bible. One example is in the Apostle Paul's first letter to the

which makes our boldest tempters uneasy. But fortunately it is quite invisible to these humans. All your patient sees is the half-finished, sham Gothic erection on the new building estate.[1] When he goes inside, he sees the local grocer with rather an oily expression on his face bustling up to offer him one shiny little book[2] containing a liturgy which neither of them understands, and one shabby little book[3] containing corrupt texts of a number of religious lyrics, mostly bad, and in very small print. When he gets to his pew and looks round him he sees just that selection of his neighbours whom he has hitherto avoided. You want to lean pretty heavily on those neighbours. Make his mind flit to and fro between an expression like "the body of Christ"[4] and the actual faces in the next pew. It matters very little, of course, what kind of people that next pew really contains. You may know one of them to be a great warrior on the Enemy's side. No matter. Your patient, thanks to Our Father Below, is a fool. Provided that any of those neighbours sing out of tune, or have boots that squeak, or double chins, or odd clothes, the patient will quite easily believe that their religion must therefore be somehow ridiculous.[5] At his present stage, you see, he has an idea of "Christians" in his mind which he supposes to be spiritual but which, in fact, is largely pictorial. His mind is full of togas and sandals and armour and bare legs[6] and the mere fact that the other people in church wear modern clothes is a real—though of course an unconscious—difficulty to him. Never let it come to the surface; never let him ask what he expected them to look like. Keep everything hazy in his mind now, and you will have all eternity wherein to amuse yourself by producing in him the peculiar kind of clarity which Hell affords.

Work hard, then, on the disappointment[7] or anticlimax which is certainly coming to the patient during his first few weeks as a churchman. The Enemy allows this disappointment to occur on the threshold of every human endeavour. It occurs when the boy who has been enchanted in the nursery by *Stories from the Odyssey*[8] buckles down to really learning Greek. It occurs when lovers have got married and begin the real task of learning to live together. In every department of life it marks the transition from

Corinthians, chapter 12, verse 27: "Now ye are the body of Christ, and members in particular," and another is in Paul's letter to the Romans, chapter 12, verses 4 and 5: "For as we have many members in one body, and all members have not the same office: so we, being many are one body in Christ and every one members one of another." (Quoted from the King James Version, which would have been commonly used in the Church of England at the time *The Screwtape Letters* was written.)

5. In Question 16 in "Answers to Questions on Christianity," Lewis recalls his own churchgoing experience as a new Christian: "I disliked very much their hymns, which I considered to be fifth-rate poems set to sixth-rate music. But as I went on I saw the great merit of it. I came up against different people of quite different outlooks and different education, and then gradually my conceit just began peeling off. I realized that the hymns (which were just sixth-rate music) were, nevertheless, being sung with devotion and benefit by an old saint in elastic-side boots in the opposite pew, and then you realize you aren't fit to clean those boots." (*God in the Dock*.)

6. Lewis is evoking the image of Christians as they would have appeared in the first century—images popularized through fiction, Passion plays, and motion pictures.

7. "Now Faith . . . is the art of holding on to things your reason has once accepted, in spite of your changing moods. I know that by experience." (*Mere Christianity,* bk. 3, chap. 11.)

8. Homer's classic *The Odyssey* was introduced and retold in *Stories from the Odyssey* by Herbert Lord Havell (1863–1918), classicist and writer. Originally published in 1908, it quickly became a mainstay of children's libraries throughout the United Kingdom.

9. A concept found throughout the Bible and, as a specific example, in the Apostle Paul's letter to the Romans, chapter 8, beginning at verse 16: "The Spirit itself beareth witness with our spirit, that we are the children of God: and if children, then heirs, heirs of God, and joint-heirs with Christ: if so be that we suffer with him, that we may be also glorified together."

10. In *The World's Last Night,* Lewis writes, "It is quite impossible—even physically impossible—to maintain any emotion for very long. Feelings come and go, and when they come a good use can be made of them: they cannot be our regular spiritual diet." The volatile nature of feelings—and the tempter's use of them against the patient—is addressed again in these letters.

11. Screwtape further explores the idea of peaks and troughs in "Letter 8" (p. 45).

dreaming aspiration to laborious doing. The Enemy takes this risk because He has a curious fantasy of making all these disgusting little human vermin into what He calls His "free" lovers and servants—"sons" is the word He uses,[9] with His inveterate love of degrading the whole spiritual world by unnatural liaisons with the two-legged animals. Desiring their freedom, He therefore refuses to carry them, by their mere affections and habits, to any of the goals which He sets before them: He leaves them to "do it on their own." And there lies our opportunity. But also, remember, there lies our danger. If once they get through this initial dryness successfully, they become much less dependent on emotion[10] and therefore much harder to tempt.[11]

I have been writing hitherto on the assumption that the people in the next pew afford no *rational* ground for disappointment. Of course if they do—if the patient knows that the woman with the absurd hat is a fanatical bridge-player or the man with squeaky boots a miser and an extortioner—then your task is so much the easier. All you then have to do is to keep out of his mind the question "If I, being what I am, can consider that I am in some sense a Christian, why should the different vices of those people in the next pew prove that their religion is mere hypocrisy and convention?" You may ask whether it is possible to keep such an obvious thought from occurring even to a human mind. It is, Wormwood, it is! Handle him properly and it simply won't come into his head. He has not been anything like long enough with the Enemy to have any real humility yet. What he says, even on his knees, about his own sinfulness is all parrot talk. At bottom, he still believes he has run up a very favourable credit-balance in the Enemy's ledger by allowing himself to be converted, and thinks that he is showing great humility and condescension in going to church with these "smug," commonplace neighbours at all. Keep him in that state of mind as long as you can.[12]

Your affectionate uncle
Screwtape

12. "As long as a man is . . . thinking of claims and counter-claims between himself and God—he is not yet in the right relation to Him. He is misunderstanding what he is and what God is. And he cannot get into the right relation until he has discovered the fact of our bankruptcy." (*Mere Christianity,* bk. 3, chap. 12.)

Letter 3

My dear Wormwood,

 am very pleased by what you tell me about this man's relations with his mother.[1] But you must press your advantage. The Enemy will be working from the centre outwards, gradually bringing more and more of the patient's conduct under the new standard,[2] and may reach his behaviour to the old lady at any moment. You want to get in first. Keep in close touch with our colleague Glubose who is in charge of the mother, and build up between you in that house a good settled habit of mutual annoyance; daily pinpricks. The following methods are useful.

Keep his mind on the inner life. He thinks his conversion is something *inside* him and his attention is therefore chiefly turned at present to the states of his own mind—or

First published in *The Guardian* on May 16, 1941.

1. Though C. S. Lewis's mother died when he was nine, he wound up with a second "mother" in Janie King "Minto" Moore. Minto was the mother of a friend—Paddy Moore—who had been killed in World War I. Lewis had promised Paddy that he'd look after Minto, should anything happen. Lewis kept that promise until Minto's death in 1951, and some biographers believe she gave Lewis the inspiration for this fictional relationship between the patient and his mother.

2. "'Make no mistake,' He says, 'if you let me, I will make you perfect. The moment you put yourself in My hands, that is what you are in for. Nothing less, or other, than that.'" (*Mere Christianity,* bk. 4, chap. 9.)

3. In chapter 14 of *Surprised By Joy*, Lewis writes, "The surest means of disarming an anger or a lust was to turn your attention from the girl or the insult and start examining the passion itself. The surest way of spoiling a pleasure was to start examining your satisfaction. But if so, it followed that all introspection is in one respect misleading. In introspection we try to look 'inside ourselves' and to see what is going on. But nearly everything that was going on a moment before is stopped by the very act of our turning to look at it. Unfortunately this does not mean that introspection finds nothing. On the contrary, it finds precisely what is left behind by the suspension of all our normal activities; and what is left behind is mainly mental images and physical sensation. The great error is to mistake this mere sediment or track or by-product for the activities themselves."

rather to that very expurgated version of them which is all you should allow him to see.[3] Encourage this. Keep his mind off the most elementary duties by directing it to the most advanced and spiritual ones. Aggravate that most useful human characteristic, the horror and neglect of the obvious. You must bring him to a condition in which he can practice self-examination for an hour without discovering any of those facts about himself which are perfectly clear to anyone who has ever lived in the same house with him or worked in the same office.

It is, no doubt, impossible to prevent his praying for his mother, but we have means of rendering the prayers innocuous. Make sure that they are always very "spiritual," that he is always concerned with the state of her soul and never with her rheumatism. Two advantages will follow. In the first place, his attention will be kept on what he regards as her sins, by which, with a little guidance from you, he can be induced to mean any of her actions which are inconvenient or irritating to himself. Thus you can keep rubbing the wounds of the day a little sorer even while he is on his knees; the operation is not at all difficult and you

16 • C.S. LEWIS

will find it very entertaining. In the second place, since his ideas about her soul will be very crude and often erroneous, he will, in some degree, be praying for an imaginary person, and it will be your task to make that imaginary person daily less and less like the real mother—the sharp-tongued old lady at the breakfast table. In time, you may get the cleavage so wide that no thought or feeling from his prayers for the imagined mother will ever flow over into his treatment of the real one. I have had patients of my own so well in hand that they could be turned at a moment's notice from impassioned prayer for a wife's or son's "soul" to beating or insulting the real wife or son without a qualm.

When two humans have lived together for many years it usually happens that each has tones of voice and expressions of face which are almost unendurably irritating to the other. Work on that. Bring fully into the consciousness of your patient that particular lift of his mother's eyebrows which he learned to dislike in the nursery, and let him think how much he dislikes it. Let him assume that she knows how annoying it is and does it to annoy—if you know your job he will not notice the immense

4. In a diary entry, Warnie recalled a letter Lewis had written to a friend three months after Janie King "Minto" Moore's death in which Lewis lamented, "I have lived most of [my private life] in a house which was hardly ever at peace for twenty-four hours, amid senseless wranglings, lyings, backbitings, follies, and *scares*. I never went home without a feeling of terror as to what appalling situation might have developed in my absence. Only now that it is over do I begin to realize quite how bad it was." (*Brothers and Friends*.) For two opposing views on the role of Janie King "Minto" Moore in C. S. Lewis's life, readers are encouraged to examine *Jack: C. S. Lewis and His Times* by George Sayer and the W. H. Lewis's *Brothers and Friends: The Diaries of Major Warren Hamilton Lewis* (specifically the entries of December 21, 1933, and January 17, 1951).

improbability of the assumption. And, of course, never let him suspect that he has tones and looks which similarly annoy her. As he cannot see or hear himself, this is easily managed.

In civilised life domestic hatred[4] usually expresses itself by saying things which would appear quite harmless on paper (the *words* are not offensive) but in such a voice, or at such a moment, that they are not far short of a blow in the face. To keep this game up you and Glubose must see to it that each of these two fools has a sort of double standard. Your patient must demand that all his own utterances are to be taken at their face value and judged simply on the actual words, while at the same time judging all his mother's utterances with the fullest and most over-sensitive interpretation of the tone and the context and the suspected intention. She must be encouraged to do the same to him. Hence from every quarrel they can both go away convinced, or very nearly convinced, that they are quite innocent. You know the kind of thing: "I simply ask her what time dinner will be and she flies into a temper." Once this habit is well established you have the delightful situation of a human saying things with the express purpose of offending and yet having a grievance when offence is taken.

Finally, tell me something about the old lady's religious position. Is she at all jealous of the new factor in her son's life?[5]—at all piqued that he should have learned from others, and so late, what she considers she gave him such good opportunity of learning in childhood? Does she feel he is making a great deal of "fuss" about it[6]—or that he's getting in on very easy terms? Remember the elder brother in the Enemy's story.[7]

Your affectionate uncle
Screwtape

5. In Walter Hooper's short biography of her, he writes, "Mrs. Moore was an atheist. She blamed God for Paddy's death." He quotes Warnie's diaries about how much she nagged Lewis about becoming a Christian. And she "chided both of them for going to those 'blood feasts' in their parish church every Sunday morning." (*Lewis: A Complete Guide,* chap. 8.)

6. In answer to Question 16 in "Answers to Questions on Christianity," Lewis notes, "It is extraordinary how inconvenient to your family it becomes for you to get up early to go to Church. It doesn't matter so much if you get up early for anything else, but if you get up early to go to Church it's very selfish of you and you upset the house." (*God in the Dock.*)

7. Screwtape is referencing a passage from the Gospel of Luke, chapter 15, in which Jesus tells the parable commonly known as The Prodigal Son. The "elder brother" in the story, who had remained faithful to his father, was angry that the father had readily welcomed home the wayward younger son, and had even thrown a feast for him.

Letter 4

My dear Wormwood,

First published in *The Guardian* on May 23, 1941.

The amateurish suggestions in your last letter warn me that it is high time for me to write to you fully on the painful subject of prayer. You might have spared the comment that my advice about his prayers for his mother "proved singularly unfortunate." That is not the sort of thing that a nephew should write to his uncle— nor a junior tempter to the under-secretary of a department. It also reveals an unpleasant desire to shift responsibility; you must learn to pay for your own blunders.

The best thing, where it is possible, is to keep the patient from the serious intention of praying altogether. When the patient is an adult recently re-converted to the Enemy's party, like your man, this is best done

1. Samuel Taylor Coleridge (1772–1834) was an English poet and literary critic. He is best known for his poems "The Rime of the Ancient Mariner" and "Kubla Khan." With William Wordsworth, he founded the Romantic movement. C. S. Lewis respected the works of Coleridge and the Romantic movement's emphasis on joy, longing, and imagination, but rejected many of their conclusions and excesses. For more on this, I recommend Wayne Martindale's essay "Romantics" in *Reading the Classics with C. S. Lewis,* edited by Thomas L. Martin (Grand Rapids, MI: Baker Academic, 2000). And, of course, Lewis himself articulates his thoughts on the subject in *Surprised By Joy.*

2. Lewis is quoting Coleridge's poem "The Pains of Sleep" (published in 1816), which begins with:

Ere on my bed my limbs I lay,
It hath not been my use to pray
With moving lips or bended knees;
But silently, by slow degrees,
My spirit I to Love compose,
In humble trust mine eye-lids close,
With reverential resignation,
No wish conceived, no thought exprest,
Only a sense of supplication;
A sense o'er all my soul imprest
That I am weak, yet not unblest,
Since in me, round me, every where
Eternal Strength and Wisdom are.

3. "For many years after my conversion I never used any ready-made forms except the Lord's Prayer. In fact I tried to pray without words at all—not to verbalize the

by encouraging him to remember, or to think he remembers, the parrot-like nature of his prayers in childhood. In reaction against that, he may be persuaded to aim at something entirely spontaneous, inward, informal, and unregularised; and what this will actually mean to a beginner will be an effort to produce in himself a vaguely devotional *mood* in which real concentration of will and intelligence have no part. One of their poets, Coleridge,[1] has recorded that he did not pray "with moving lips and bended knees" but merely "composed his spirit to love" and indulged "a sense of supplication."[2] That is exactly the sort of prayer we want; and since it bears a superficial resemblance to the prayer of silence as practised by those who are very far advanced in the Enemy's service, clever and lazy patients can be taken in by it for quite a long time.[3] At the very least, they can be persuaded that the bodily position makes no difference to their prayers; for they constantly forget, what you must always remember, that they are animals and that whatever their bodies do affects their souls.[4] It is funny how mortals always picture us as putting things into their minds: in reality our best work is done by keeping things out.

If this fails, you must fall back on a subtler misdirection of his intention. Whenever they are attending to the Enemy Himself we are defeated, but there are ways of preventing them from doing so. The simplest is to turn their gaze away from Him towards themselves.[5] Keep them watching their own minds[6] and trying to produce *feelings* there by the action of their own wills.[7] When they meant to ask Him for charity, let them, instead, start trying to manufacture charitable feelings for themselves and not notice that this is what they are doing. When they meant to pray for courage, let them really be trying to feel brave. When they say they are praying for forgiveness, let them be trying to feel forgiven. Teach them to estimate the value of each prayer by their success in producing the desired feeling; and never let them suspect how much success or failure of that kind depends on whether they are well or ill, fresh or tired, at the moment.[8]

But of course the Enemy will not meantime be idle. Wherever there is prayer, there

mental acts. . . . I still think the prayer without words is the best—if one can really achieve it. But I now see that in trying to make it my daily bread I was counting on a greater mental and spiritual strength than I really have." (*Letters to Malcolm,* chap. 2.)

4. Lewis echoes this idea in chapter 3 of *Letters to Malcolm*: "When one prays in strange places and at strange times one can't kneel, to be sure. I won't say this doesn't matter. The body ought to pray as well as the soul. Body and soul are both the better for it. . . . The relevant point is that kneeling does matter, but other things matter even more. A concentrated mind and a sitting body make for better prayer than a kneeling body and a mind half asleep." In chapter 5 of *Mere Christianity*, Lewis writes, "Christianity is almost the only one of the great religions which thoroughly approves of the body—which believes that matter is good, that God Himself once took on a human body, that some kind of body is going to be given to us even in Heaven and is going to be an essential part of our happiness, our beauty, and our energy."

5. In a letter dated July 31, 1954, Lewis wrote that one of his own rules about prayer was "to avoid introspection in prayer—I mean not to *watch* one's own mind to see if it is in the right frame, but always to turn the attention outward to God." (*Collected Letters III.*)

6. In book 3, chapter 12 of *Mere Christianity*, Lewis writes, "Do not sit down and start watching your own mind to see if it is coming along. That puts a man quite on the wrong track. When the most important things in our life happen we quite often do not know, at the moment, what is going on."

7. Lewis experienced that very thing as a child after learning of his mother's cancer. "When her case was pronounced hopeless I remembered what I had been taught; that prayers offered in faith would be granted. I accordingly set myself to produce by will-power a firm belief that my prayers for her recovery would be successful." (*Surprised By Joy*, chap. 1.) Much later in his life, Lewis reiterated that idea: "We must not encourage ourselves or others any tendency to work up a subjective state which, if we succeeded, we should describe as 'faith,' with the idea that this will somehow ensure the granting of our prayer. We have probably all done this as children. But the state of mind which desperate desire working on a strong imagination can manufacture is not faith in the Christian sense. It is a feat of psychological gymnastics." (*Letters to Malcolm*, chap. 11.)

8. In a letter to Mrs. Frank L. Jones, dated February 23, 1947, Lewis wrote, "God [could], had he pleased, have been incarnate in a man of iron nerves, the Stoic sort who lets no sigh escape Him. Of His great humility He chose to be incarnate in a man of delicate sensibilities who wept at the grave of Lazarus and sweated blood in Gethsemane. Otherwise we should have missed the great lesson that it is by his

is danger of His own immediate action. He is cynically indifferent to the dignity of His position, and ours, as pure spirits, and to human animals on their knees He pours out self-knowledge in a quite shameless fashion. But even if He defeats your first attempt at misdirection, we have a subtler weapon. The humans do not start from that direct perception of Him which we, unhappily, cannot avoid. They have never known that ghastly luminosity, that stabbing and searing glare which makes the background of permanent pain to our lives. If you look into your patient's mind when he is praying, you will not find that. If you examine the object to which he is attending, you will find that it is a composite object containing many quite ridiculous ingredients. There will be images derived from pictures of the Enemy as He appeared during the discreditable episode known as the Incarnation:[9] there will be vaguer—perhaps quite savage and puerile—images associated with the other two Persons.[10] There will even be some of his own reverence (and of bodily sensations accompanying it) objectified and attributed to the object revered. I have known cases where what the patient called his "God" was actually *located*—up and to the left at the corner of the bedroom ceiling, or inside his own head, or in a crucifix on the wall.[11] But whatever the nature of the composite object, you must keep him praying to *it*—to the thing that he has made, not to the Person who has made him. You may even encourage him to attach great importance to the correction and improvement of his composite object, and to keeping it steadily before his imagination during the whole prayer. For if he ever comes to make the distinction, if ever he consciously directs his prayers "Not to what I think thou art but to what thou knowest thyself to be,"[12] our situation is, for the moment, desperate. Once all his thoughts and images have been flung aside or, if retained, retained with a full recognition of their merely subjective nature, and the man trusts himself to the completely real, external, invisible Presence, there with him in the room and never knowable by him as he is known by it— why, then it is that the incalculable may occur.[13] In avoiding this situation—this real nakedness of the soul in prayer—you

will alone that a man is good or bad, and that *feelings* are not, in themselves, of any importance." (*Collected Letters II.*)

9. "The Enemy as He appeared during . . . the Incarnation" is referencing Jesus Christ who, according to Christian belief, is God incarnate (in the flesh).

10. "The other two Persons" is referring to God the Father and God the Holy Spirit— the other two persons in the Trinity with Jesus Christ.

11. "The Teddy Bear exists in order that the child may endow it with imaginary life and personality and enter into a quasi-social relationship with it. That is what 'play with it' means. The better this activity succeeds the less the actual appearance of the object will matter. Too close or prolonged attention to its changeless and expressionless face impedes the play. A crucifix exists in order to direct the worshipper's thought and affections to the Passion. It had better not have any excellencies, subtleties, or originalities which will fix attention upon itself. Hence devout people may, for this purpose, prefer the crudest and emptiest icon. The emptier, the more permeable; and they want, as it were, to pass through the material image and go beyond." (*Experiment in Criticism*, "How the Few and the Many Use Pictures and Music.")

12. "The prayer preceding all prayers is, 'May it be the real I who speaks. May it be the real Thou that I speak to.' Infinitely various are the levels from which we pray.

Emotional intensity is in itself no proof of spiritual depth. If we pray in terror we shall pray earnestly; it only proves that terror is an earnest emotion. Only God Himself can let the bucket down to the depths in us. And, on the other side, he must constantly work as the iconoclast. Every idea of Him we form, he must in mercy shatter." (*Letters to Malcolm,* chap. 15.)

13. "The two facades—the 'I' as I perceive myself and the room as I perceive it— were obstacles as long as I mistook them for ultimate realities. But the moment I recognized them as facades, as mere surfaces, they became conductors. . . . The objects around me, and my idea of 'me,' will deceive if taken at their face value. But they are momentous if taken as the end-products of divine activities. Thus and not otherwise, the creation of matter and the creation of mind meet one another and the circuit is closed." (*Letters to Malcolm,* chap. 15.)

14. For Lewis's perspective on prayer, it is worth reading his *Letters to Malcolm, Chiefly on Prayer*; "The Efficacy of Prayer" in *The World's Last Night and Other Essays*; *Letters to an American Lady*; "Petitionary Prayer: A Problem Without an Answer" in *Christian Reflections*; and "Work and Prayer" in *God in the Dock.*

will be helped by the fact that the humans themselves do not desire it as much as they suppose. There's such a thing as getting more than they bargained for![14]

Your affectionate uncle
Screwtape

Letter 5

My dear Wormwood,

First published in *The Guardian* on May 30, 1941.

I t is a little bit disappointing to expect a detailed report on your work and to receive instead such a vague rhapsody as your last letter. You say you are "delirious with joy" because the European humans have started another of their wars. I see very well what has happened to you. You are not delirious; you are only drunk. Reading between the lines in your very unbalanced account of the patient's sleepless night, I can reconstruct your state of mind fairly accurately. For the first time in your career you have tasted that wine which is the reward of all our labours—the anguish and bewilderment of a human soul—and it has gone to your head. I can hardly blame you. I do not expect old heads on young shoulders. Did the patient respond to some of your terror-pictures of the future? Did you work in some good self-pitying glances at the happy past?—some fine thrills in the pit of his stomach, were there? You played your violin prettily, did you? Well, well, it's all very natural. But do remember, Wormwood, that duty comes before pleasure. If any present self-indulgence on your part leads to the ultimate loss of the prey, you will be left eternally thirsting for that draught of which you are now so much enjoying your first sip. If, on the other hand, by steady and coolheaded application here and now you can finally secure his soul, he will then be yours forever—a brim-full living chalice of despair and horror and astonishment which you can raise to your lips as often as you please. So do not allow any temporary excitement to distract you from the real business of undermining faith and preventing the formation of virtues. Give me without fail in your next letter a full account of the patient's reactions to the war, so that we can consider whether you are likely to do more good by making him an extreme patriot or an ardent pacifist. There are all sorts of possibilities. In the meantime, I must warn you not to hope too much from a war.

Of course a war is entertaining. The immediate fear and suffering of the humans is a legitimate and pleasing refreshment for our myriads of toiling workers. But what permanent good does it do us unless we make use of it for bringing souls to Our Father Below? When I see the temporal suffering of humans who finally escape us, I feel as if I had been allowed to taste the first course of a rich banquet and then denied the rest. It is worse than not to have tasted it at all. The Enemy, true to His barbarous methods of warfare, allows us to see the short misery of His favourites only to tantalise and torment us—to mock the incessant hunger which, during this present phase of the great conflict,[1] His blockade is admittedly imposing. Let us therefore think rather how to use, than how to enjoy, this European war.[2] For it has certain tendencies inherent in it which are, in themselves, by no means in our favour. We may hope for a good deal of cruelty and unchastity. But, if we are not careful, we shall see thousands turning in this tribulation to the Enemy, while tens of thousands who do not go so far as that will nevertheless have their attention diverted from themselves to values and causes which they

1. "The great conflict" evokes the apocalyptic images and references found in the books of Daniel and Isaiah in the Old Testament of the Bible, as well as the book of Revelation at the end of the New Testament. John Milton's *Paradise Lost* also records the great conflict after the rebellion by Satan and other angels before the Fall of Humanity (as recorded in the book of Genesis). This conflict between God and Satan will continue until the end of time.

2. At the time of writing, this truly was the "European war" since neither the United States nor Japan had joined it.

3. Lewis further explores this idea in *The Chronicles of Narnia,* at the end of *The Last Battle,* as Emeth of Calormen is welcomed by Aslan even though Emeth had spent his life serving the god Tash. Aslan states to Emeth, "Child, all the service thou hast done to Tash, I account as service done to me. . . . No service which is vile can be done to me, and none which is not vile can be done to him. Therefore if any man swear by Tash and keep his oath for the oath's sake, it is by me that he has truly sworn, though he know it not, and it is I who reward him. And if any man do a cruelty in my name, then, though he says the name Aslan, it is Tash whom he serves and by Tash his deed is accepted." (*Last Battle,* chap. 15.)

4. In "Learning in War-Time" Lewis observes, "War makes death real to us, and that would have been regarded as one of its blessings by most of the great Christians of the past. They thought it good for us to be always aware of our mortality. I am inclined to think they were right." (*Weight of Glory.*)

5. In a letter to his friend Arthur Greeves, dated September 15, 1939, Lewis wrote, "The next few years will be ghastly, but though my *nerves* are often staggered, my faith and reason are alright. I have no doubt that all this suffering will be for our ultimate good if we use it rightly . . . but I can't help wishing one could *hibernate* till it's all over! . . . I daresay for me, personally, it has come in the nick of time: I was just beginning to get too well settled in my

believe to be higher than the self. I know that the Enemy disapproves many of these causes. But that is where He is so unfair. He often makes prizes of humans who have given their lives for causes He thinks bad on the monstrously sophistical ground that the humans thought them good and were following the best they knew.[3] Consider too what undesirable deaths occur in wartime. Men are killed in places where they knew they might be killed and to which they go, if they are at all of the Enemy's party, prepared. How much better for us if all humans died in costly nursing homes amid doctors who lie, nurses who lie, friends who lie, as we have trained them, promising life to the dying, encouraging the belief that sickness excuses every indulgence, and even, if our workers know their job, withholding all suggestion of a priest lest it should betray to the sick man his true condition! And how disastrous for us is the continual remembrance of death which war enforces.[4] One of our best weapons, contented worldliness, is rendered useless.[5] In wartime not even a human can believe that he is going to live forever.

I know that Scabtree and others have seen in wars a great opportunity for attacks on faith, but I think that view was exaggerated. The Enemy's human partisans have all been plainly told by Him that suffering is an essential part of what He calls Redemption;[6] so that a faith which is destroyed by a war or a pestilence cannot really have been worth the trouble of destroying. I am speaking now of diffused suffering over a long period such as the war will produce. Of course, at the precise moment of terror, bereavement, or physical pain, you may catch your man when his reasons temporarily suspended. But even then, if he applies to Enemy headquarters, I have found that the post is nearly always defended,

Your affectionate uncle
Screwtape

profession, too successful, and probably self complacent." (*Collected Letters II.*)

6. "If the first and lowest operation of pain shatters the illusion that all is well, the second shatters the illusion that what we have, whether good or bad in itself, is our own and enough for us. Everyone has noticed how hard it is to turn our thoughts to God when everything is going well with us." (*Problem of Pain*, chap. 6.)

Letter 6

My dear Wormwood,

I am delighted to hear that your patient's age and profession make it possible, but by no means certain, that he will be called up for military service.[1] We want him to be in the maximum uncertainty, so that his mind will be filled with contradictory pictures of the future, every one of which arouses hope or fear. There is nothing like suspense and anxiety for barricading a human's mind against the Enemy. He wants men to be concerned with what they do; our business is to keep them thinking about what will happen to them.

Your patient will, of course, have picked up the notion that he must submit with patience to the Enemy's will. What the Enemy means by this is primarily that he should accept with patience the tribulation

First published in *The Guardian* on June 6, 1941.

1. Lewis knew firsthand what this felt like. At the start of World War II, he was forty years old and still eligible to be called up for military duty.

2. In a letter dated October 20, 1957, Lewis advised his friend about dealing with pain: "The great thing . . . is to live from day to day and hour to hour not adding the past or future to the present. . . . In fact, as Our Lord said, 'Sufficient unto the day.'" (*Letters to an American Lady.*)

3. References the words of Jesus in the Gospels. See Matthew, chapter 6, verse 10, in which Jesus teaches the Lord's Prayer and, specifically, the phrase "Thy kingdom come, Thy will be done on earth as it is in heaven." Also, in the Garden of Gethsemane, Jesus prays that God will save Him from His forthcoming crucifixion, but concludes with "O my Father, if this cup may not pass away from me, except I drink it, thy will be done" (Matthew 26:36–46; Luke 22:39–46; Mark 14:32–42).

4. References another section of the Lord's Prayer (Matthew 6:11), in which Jesus teaches his disciples to pray "Give us this day our daily bread."

5. In the Gospel of Luke 9:23, Jesus states to his disciples, "If any man will come after me, let him deny himself, and take up his cross daily, and follow me." The meaning and practical application of picking up one's cross has been explored by Christian thinkers for the past two thousand years. The general concept is that an "appointed cross" is any suffering or difficulty given by God to a Christian to endure.

which has actually been dealt out to him— the present anxiety and suspense.[2] It is about *this* that he is to say "Thy will be done,"[3] and for the daily task of bearing *this* that the daily bread[4] will be provided. It is your business to see that the patient never thinks of the present fear as his appointed cross[5] but only of the things he is afraid of. Let him regard them as his crosses: let him forget that, since they are incompatible, they cannot all happen to him, and let him try to practise fortitude and patience to them all in advance. For real resignation, at the same moment, to a dozen different and hypothetical fates, is almost impossible, and the Enemy does not greatly assist those who are trying to attain it: resignation to present and actual suffering, even where that suffering consists of fear, is far easier and is usually helped by this direct action.

An important spiritual law is here involved. I have explained that you can weaken his prayers by diverting his attention from the Enemy Himself to his own states of mind about the Enemy. On the other hand fear becomes easier to master when the patient's mind is diverted from the thing feared to the fear itself, considered as a present and undesirable state of his own mind; and when he regards the fear as his appointed cross he will inevitably think of it as a state of mind. One can therefore formulate the general rule; in all activities of mind which favour our cause, encourage the patient to be unselfconscious and to concentrate on the object, but in all activities favourable to the Enemy bend his mind back on itself. Let an insult or a woman's body so fix his attention outward that he does not reflect "I am now entering into the state called Anger—or the state called Lust." Contrariwise let the reflection "My feelings are now growing more devout, or more charitable" so fix his attention inward that he no longer looks beyond himself to see our Enemy or his own neighbours.

As regards his more general attitude to the war, you must not rely too much on those feelings of hatred which the humans are so fond of discussing in Christian, or anti-Christian, periodicals. In his anguish, the patient can, of course, be encouraged to revenge himself by some vindictive feelings directed towards the German leaders, and that is good so far as it goes. But it is usually a sort of melodramatic or mythical hatred directed against imaginary scape-goats. He has never met these people in real life—they are lay figures modelled on what he gets from newspapers. The results of such fanciful hatred are often most disappointing, and of all humans the English are in this respect the most deplorable milksops.[6] They are creatures of that miserable sort who loudly proclaim that torture is too good for their enemies and then give tea and cigarettes to the first wounded German pilot who turns up at the back door.[7]

Do what you will, there is going to be some benevolence, as well as some malice, in your patient's soul. The great thing is to direct the malice to his immediate neighbours whom he meets every day and to thrust his benevolence out to the remote circumference, to people he does not know. The malice thus becomes wholly real and the benevolence largely imaginary. There is no good at all in inflaming his hatred of Germans if, at the same time, a pernicious habit of charity is growing up between him and his mother, his employer, and the man he meets in the train. Think of your man as a series of concentric circles, his will being the innermost, his intellect coming next, and finally his fantasy. You can hardly hope, at once, to exclude from all the circles everything that smells of the Enemy: but you must keep on shoving all the virtues[8] outward till they are finally located in the circle of fantasy, and all the desirable qualities inward into the Will. It is only in so far as they reach the will and are there embodied in habits that the virtues are really fatal to us. (I don't, of course, mean what the patient mistakes for his will, the conscious fume and fret of resolutions and clenched teeth, but the real centre, what the Enemy calls the Heart.) All sorts of virtues painted in the fantasy or approved by the intellect or even, in some measure, loved and admired, will not keep a man from our Father's house: indeed they may make him more amusing when he gets there,

Your affectionate uncle
Screwtape

8. In traditional Christianity, "cardinal" or "natural" virtues include prudence, temperance, fortitude, and justice; the "theological" virtues include faith, hope, and charity (love). Lewis writes extensively about the virtues in book 3, chapter 2, of *Mere Christianity*.

Letter 7

My dear Wormwood,

First published in *The Guardian* on June 13, 1941.

I wonder you should ask me whether it is essential to keep the patient in ignorance of your own existence. That question, at least for the present phase of the struggle, has been answered for us by the High Command. Our policy, for the moment, is to conceal ourselves. Of course this has not always been so. We are really faced with a cruel dilemma. When the humans disbelieve in our existence we lose all the pleasing results of direct terrorism and we make no magicians. On the other hand, when they believe in us, we cannot make them materialists and skeptics. At least, not yet. I have great hopes that we shall learn in due time how to emotionalise and mythologise their science to such an extent that what is, in effect, a belief in us (though not under

1. Lewis is referencing the writings of French philosopher Henri-Louis Bergson (1859–1941) and playwright George Bernard Shaw (1856–1950) who, independent of one another and using different terms, both postulated on the concept of a benign "Life Force," or a creative consciousness, that guides man, by trial and error, through evolution. Bergson won the Nobel Prize in Literature in 1927 for his work *The Creative Evolution,* which captured this view as what he called "elan vital." Shaw explored similar ideas in his 1903 play *Man and Superman* and in his 1921 five-play cycle *Back to Methuselah.* Lewis tackled creative evolution and the life force in book 1, chapter 4 of *Mere Christianity* and chapter 5 of *The Four Loves.* He also takes another jab at creative evolution in "Letter 15" (p. 87) and at George Bernard Shaw in "Letter 22" (p. 129).

2. Lewis touches on materialist magicians in his other fictional works. Professor Weston in *Perelandra* and Uncle Andrew in *The Magician's Nephew* could both be considered materialist magicians.

3. In logic or rhetoric, this is a classic fallacy or, as some would call it, a red herring (a sneaky diversion). It diverts an argument or opinion away from the actual point to something related, but irrelevant, in order to keep the validity of the argument or opinion from being truly tested. Screwtape uses this technique repeatedly. Lewis himself also developed a version of this technique called bulverism. In an essay of that same name in *God in the Dock,* he explains, "You must show *that* a

that name) will creep in while the human mind remains closed to belief in the Enemy. The "Life Force,"[1] the worship of sex, and some aspects of Psychoanalysis, may here prove useful. If once we can produce our perfect work—the Materialist Magician,[2] the man, not using, but veritably worshipping, what he vaguely calls "Forces" while denying the existence of "spirits"—then the end of the war will be in sight. But in the meantime we must obey our orders. I do not think you will have much difficulty in keeping the patient in the dark. The fact that "devils" are predominantly *comic* figures in the modern imagination will help you. If any faint suspicion of your existence begins to arise in his mind, suggest to him a picture of something in red tights, and persuade him that since he cannot believe in that (it is an old textbook method of confusing them) he therefore cannot believe in you.[3]

I had not forgotten my promise to consider whether we should make the patient an extreme patriot or an extreme pacifist.[4] All extremes, except extreme devotion to the Enemy, are to be encouraged. Not always, of course, but at this period.

Some ages are lukewarm and complacent, and then it is our business to soothe them yet faster asleep. Other ages, of which the present is one, are unbalanced and prone to faction, and it is our business to inflame them. Any small coterie,[5] bound together by some interest which other men dislike or ignore, tends to develop inside itself a hothouse mutual admiration, and towards the outer world, a great deal of pride and hatred which is entertained without shame because the "Cause" is its sponsor and it is thought to be impersonal. Even when the little group exists originally for the Enemy's own purposes, this remains true. We want the Church to be small not only that fewer men may know the Enemy but also that those who do may acquire the uneasy intensity and the defensive self-righteousness of a secret society or a clique. The Church herself is, of course, heavily defended and we have never yet quite succeeded in giving her *all* the characteristics of a faction; but subordinate factions within her have often produced admirable results, from the parties of Paul and of Apollos at Corinth[6] down to the High and Low parties in the Church of England.[7]

man is wrong before you start explaining *why* he is wrong. The modern method is to assume without discussion *that* he is wrong and then distract his attention from this (the only real issue) by busily explaining how he became so silly." (*God in the Dock*.)

4. It is worth reading Lewis's view on patriotism and pacifism in his essay "Why I Am Not a Pacifist" in *The Weight of Glory*.

5. Lewis warns of the dangerous tendency for groups, which formed for positive reasons, to become coteries that exist primarily for the pleasure of excluding others, "a little self-elected . . . aristocracy, basking in the moonshine of our collective self-approval." (*Four Loves*, chap. 4.)

6. "Paul" is referring to the Apostle Paul, and "Apollos" is referring to an Alexandrian Jew of that same period who became a Christian and evangelized in Ephesus and Achaia (Acts 18:24–28). Apollos's understanding of baptism was based on the call to repentance from John the Baptist and was incomplete. He was eventually brought up to date about baptism in the name of Jesus. Still, Paul had to rebaptize some believers (Acts 19:1–7). Screwtape alludes to the factional conflict mentioned in Paul's first letter to the Corinthian church. Paul reprimands the church for falling into divisions between those who followed Paul and those who followed Apollos.

7. In the Church of England, there are those who hold a "High" view of the authority of the bishops, the use of sacraments, and the practices in traditional liturgy. The "Low" view diminishes those aspects of Christianity in favor of a more nonconformist approach to church government, rites, and form.

If your patient can be induced to become a conscientious objector he will automatically find himself one of a small, vocal, organised, and unpopular society, and the effects of this, on one so new to Christianity, will almost certainly be good. But only *almost* certainly. Has he had serious doubts about the lawfulness of serving in a just war before this present war began? Is he a man of great physical courage—so great that he will have no half-conscious misgivings about the real motives of his pacifism? Can he, when nearest to honesty (no human is ever *very* near), feel fully convinced that he is actuated wholly by the desire to obey the Enemy? If he is that sort of man, his pacifism will probably not do us much good, and the Enemy will probably protect him from the usual consequences of belonging to a sect. Your best plan, in that case, would be to attempt a sudden, confused, emotional crisis from which he might emerge as an uneasy convert to patriotism. Such things can often be managed. But if he is the man I take him to be, try Pacifism.

Whichever he adopts, your main task will be the same. Let him begin by treating the Patriotism or the Pacifism as a part of his religion. Then let him, under the influence of partisan spirit, come to regard it as the most important part. Then quietly and gradually nurse him on to the stage at which the religion becomes merely part of the "cause," in which Christianity is valued chiefly because of the excellent arguments it can produce in favour of the British war-effort or of Pacifism. The attitude which you want to guard against is that in which temporal affairs are treated primarily as material for obedience. Once you have made the World an end, and faith a means, you have almost won your man, and it makes very little difference what kind of worldly end he is pursuing. Provided that meetings, pamphlets, policies, movements, causes, and crusades, matter more to him than prayers and sacraments and charity, he is ours—and the more "religious" (on those terms) the more securely ours. I could show you a pretty cageful down here,[8]

Your affectionate uncle
Screwtape

8. Lewis returns to the subject of factions at the end of *Screwtape Proposes a Toast* (p. 191).

Letter 8

My dear Wormwood,

So you "have great hopes that the patient's religious phase is dying away,"[1] have you? I always thought the Training College had gone to pieces since they put old Slubgob at the head of it, and now I am sure. Has no one ever told you about the law of Undulation?

Humans are amphibians[2]—half spirit and half animal. (The Enemy's determination to produce such a revolting hybrid was one of the things that determined Our Father to withdraw his support from Him.[3]) As spirits they belong to the eternal world, but as animals they inhabit time. This means that while their spirit can be directed to an eternal object, their bodies, passions, and imaginations are in continual change, for to be in time means to change. Their

First published in *The Guardian* on June 20, 1941.

1. "Many religious people lament that the first fervours of their conversion have died away. They think—sometimes rightly, but not, I believe always—that their sins account for this. They may even try by pitiful efforts of will to revive what now seem to have been the golden days. But were those fervours—the operative word is *those*—ever intended to last?" (*Letters to Malcolm,* chap. 5.)

2. The description of humans as "amphibians" echoes an author much admired by Lewis: Sir Thomas Browne (1605–1682), a writer, natural historian, and philosopher. In his *Religio Medici* (1643), Browne wrote, "Thus is man that great and true *Amphibium,* whose nature is disposed to live not onely like other creatures in divers elements, but in divided and distinguished worlds." So, simply put, just as a frog lives on land and in water, so humans exist in both the temporal and spiritual worlds.

3. A reference by Lewis to John Milton (1608–1674) and book 1 of his epic poem *Paradise Lost,* in which Satan and his

followers rebel and wage war against God. See also Isaiah 14:12 and Ezekiel 28:12 in the Bible which, according to Christian tradition, refer to Satan. Screwtape ascribes various motivations for Satan's rebellion, including God's creation and love for humans.

4. Lewis is likely referring to saints and mystics, such as Saint John of the Cross, who wrote *The Dark Night of the Soul.* In chapter 8 of *Letters to Malcolm,* Lewis states, "It is saints, not common people, who experience the 'dark night.' . . . The 'hiddenness' of God perhaps presses most painfully on those who are in another way nearest to Him."

nearest approach to constancy, therefore, is undulation—the repeated return to a level from which they repeatedly fall back, a series of troughs and peaks. If you had watched your patient carefully you would have seen this undulation in every department of his life—his interest in his work, his affection for his friends, his physical appetites, all go up and down. As long as he lives on earth periods of emotional and bodily richness and liveliness will alternate with periods of numbness and poverty. The dryness and dullness through which your patient is now going are not, as you fondly suppose, your workmanship; they are merely a natural phenomenon which will do us no good unless you make a good use of it.

To decide what the best use of it is, you must ask what use the Enemy wants to make of it, and then do the opposite. Now it may surprise you to learn that in His efforts to get permanent possession of a soul, He relies on the troughs even more than on the peaks; some of His special favourites[4] have gone through longer and deeper troughs than anyone else. The reason is this. To us a human is primarily food; our aim is the absorption of its will into ours, the increase of our own area of selfhood at its expense. But the obedience which the Enemy demands of men is quite a different thing. One must face the fact that all the talk about His love for men, and His service being perfect freedom, is not (as one would gladly believe) mere propaganda, but an appalling truth. He really *does* want to fill the universe with a lot of loathsome little replicas of Himself[5]—creatures whose life, on its miniature scale, will be qualitatively like His own, not because He has absorbed them but because their wills freely conform to His. We want cattle who can finally become food; He wants servants who can finally become sons. We want to suck in; He wants to give out. We are empty and would be filled; He is full and flows over. Our war aim is a world in which Our Father Below has drawn all other beings into himself:[6] the Enemy wants a world full of beings united to Him but still distinct.

And that is where the troughs come in. You must have often wondered why the Enemy does not make more use of His power to be sensibly present to human souls in any degree He chooses and at any moment. But you now see that the Irresistible and the

5. In book 4, chapter 4 of *Mere Christianity*, Lewis states, "Now the whole offer which Christianity makes is this: that we can, if we let God have His way, come to share in the life of Christ. If we do, we shall then be sharing a life which was begotten, not made, which always has existed and always will exist. Christ is the Son of God. If we share in this kind of life we also shall be sons of God. We shall love the Father as He does and the Holy Ghost will arise in us. He came to this world and became a man in order to spread to other men the kind of life He has—by what I call 'good infection.' Every Christian is to become a little Christ. The whole purpose of becoming a Christian is simply nothing else."

6. Lewis makes more of this idea in his novel *Perelandra* (London: John Lane, 1943), in which the physicist Weston becomes food for the devil and his demons. Lewis describes the ingesting as a "confusion of persons" and "what the Pantheists falsely hoped of heaven bad men really received in hell" as they were "melted down into their Master, as a lead soldier slips down and loses his shape in the ladle over the gas ring."

7. John Calvin (1509–1564) was a French theologian and significant contributor to the Protestant Reformation who promoted a view that those who became Christians were predetermined by God to do so, drawn to God by an "irresistible" and specific grace in conformity with his sovereign will, thus overriding the free will of humans. Lewis did not subscribe to this view and refuted it in various works, maintaining that humans always have a choice in their salvation or damnation. Notably, in chapter 9 of Lewis's novel *The Great Divorce* (New York: Macmillan, 1946), the character of George MacDonald says, "There are only two kinds of people in the end: those who say to God 'Thy will be done,' and those to whom God says, in the end '*thy* will be done.' All that are in Hell, choose it."

8. "God has made it a rule for Himself that He won't alter people's character by force. He can and will alter them—but only if the people will let Him. In that way He has really and truly limited His power. . . . He would rather have a world of free beings, with all its risks, than a world of people who did right like machines because they couldn't do anything else." (*God in the Dock,* "The Trouble With 'X.'")

9. In a letter dated May 2, 1945, Lewis wrote, "I believe my doctrine about troughs to be true because every good writer on the spiritual life says the same." Later, he added, "And don't forget that Our Lord Himself experienced troughs: to the point of saying 'Why hast Thou forsaken me?'" (*Collected Letters III.*)

Indisputable are the two weapons which the very nature of His scheme forbids Him to use.[7] Merely to over-ride a human will (as His felt presence in any but the faintest and most mitigated degree would certainly do) would be for Him useless.[8] He cannot ravish. He can only woo. For His ignoble idea is to eat the cake and have it; the creatures are to be one with Him, but yet themselves; merely to cancel them, or assimilate them, will not serve. He is prepared to do a little over-riding at the beginning. He will set them off with communications of His presence which, though faint, seem great to them, with emotional sweetness, and easy conquest over temptation. But He never allows this state of affairs to last long. Sooner or later He withdraws, if not in fact, at least from their conscious experience, all those supports and incentives. He leaves the creature to stand up on its own legs—to carry out from the will alone duties which have lost all relish. It is during such trough periods, much more than during the peak periods, that it is growing into the sort of creature He wants it to be.[9] Hence the prayers offered in the state of dryness are those which please Him best. We can drag our patients along by continual tempting, because we design them only for the table, and the more their will is interfered with the better. He cannot "tempt" to virtue as we do to vice. He wants them to learn to walk and must therefore take away His hand; and if only the will to walk is really there He is pleased even with their stumbles. Do not be deceived, Wormwood. Our cause is never more in danger than when a human, no longer desiring, but still intending, to do our Enemy's will, looks round upon a universe from which every trace of Him seems to have vanished, and asks why he has been forsaken, and still obeys.[10]

But of course the troughs afford opportunities to our side also. Next week[11] I will give you some hints on how to exploit them,

Your affectionate uncle
Screwtape

10. In 1948, Lewis wrote, "The Father can be well pleased in that Son only who adheres to the Father when apparently forsaken. The fullest grace can be received by those only who continue to obey during the dryness in which all grace seems to be withheld." (*Arthurian Torso.*) This view, espoused by George MacDonald, was quoted by Lewis in an anthology of MacDonald's work: "The highest condition of the Human Will, as distinct, not as separated from God, is when, not seeing God, not seeming to itself to grasp Him at all, it yet holds Him fast." Taken from "The Eloi" in *Unspoken Sermons,* vol. 1 (London: Alexander Strahan, 1867). See also the Gospel of Matthew 27:46.

11. A wry acknowledgement that the letters were weekly installments for *The Guardian.*

Letter 9

My dear Wormwood,

First published in *The Guardian* on June 27, 1941.

I hope my last letter has convinced you that the trough of dullness or "dryness" through which your patient is going at present will not, of itself, give you his soul, but needs to be properly exploited. What forms the exploitation should take I will now consider.

In the first place I have always found that the Trough periods of the human undulation provide excellent opportunity for all sensual temptations, particularly those of sex. This may surprise you, because, of course, there is more physical energy, and therefore more potential appetite, at the Peak periods; but you must remember that the powers of resistance are then also at their highest. The health and spirits which

1. Milk and water: weak, insipid, feeble.

2. Concomitants: things that accompany or occur at the same time.

3. Anodyne: a painkiller.

you want to use in producing lust can also, alas, be very easily used for work or play or thought or innocuous merriment. The attack has a much better chance of success when the man's whole inner world is drab and cold and empty. And it is also to be noted that the Trough sexuality is subtly different in quality from that of the Peak— much less likely to lead to the milk and water[1] phenomenon which the humans call "being in love," much more easily drawn into perversions, much less contaminated by those generous and imaginative and even spiritual concomitants[2] which often render human sexuality so disappointing. It is the same with other desires of the flesh. You are much more likely to make your man a sound drunkard by pressing drink on him as an anodyne[3] when he is dull and weary than by encouraging him to use it as a means of merriment among his friends when he is happy and expansive. Never forget that when we are dealing with any pleasure in its healthy and normal and satisfying form, we are, in a sense, on the Enemy's ground. I know we have won many a soul through pleasure. All the same, it is His invention, not ours. He made the pleasures: all our research so far has not enabled us to produce one. All we can do is to encourage the humans to take the pleasures which our Enemy has produced, at times, or in ways, or in degrees, which He has forbidden. Hence we always try to work away from the natural condition of any pleasure to that in which it is least natural, least redolent of its Maker, and least pleasurable. An ever increasing craving for an ever diminishing pleasure is the formula.[4] It is more certain; and it's better style. To get the man's soul and give him *nothing* in return—that is what really gladdens our Father's heart. And the troughs are the time for beginning the process.

But there is an even better way of exploiting the Trough; I mean through the patient's own thoughts about it. As always, the first step is to keep knowledge out of his mind. Do not let him suspect the law of undulation. Let him assume that the first ardours of his conversion might have been expected to last, and ought to have lasted, forever, and that his present dryness is an equally permanent condition. Having

4. In chapter 2 of *The Four Loves* Lewis echoes this point: "For the temperate man an occasional glass of wine is a treat . . . But to the alcoholic, whose palate and digestion have long since been destroyed, no liquor gives any pleasure except that of relief from an unbearable craving."

5. Lewis writes in book 3, chapter 6 of *Mere Christianity*, "It is simply no good trying to keep any thrill: that is the very worst thing you can do. Let the thrill go—let it die away—go on through that period of death into the quieter interest and happiness that follow—and you will find you are living in a world of new thrills all the time."

once got this misconception well fixed in his head, you may then proceed in various ways. It all depends on whether your man is of the desponding type who can be tempted to despair, or of the wishful-thinking type who can be assured that all is well. The former type is getting rare among the humans. If your patient should happen to belong to it, everything is easy. You have only got to keep him out of the way of experienced Christians (an easy task now-adays), to direct his attention to the appropriate passages in scripture, and then to set him to work on the desperate design of recovering his old feelings by sheer will-power, and the game is ours.[5] If he is of the more hopeful type, your job is to make him acquiesce in the present low temperature of his spirit and gradually become content with it, persuading himself that it is not so low after all. In a week or two you will be making him doubt whether the first days of his Christianity were not, perhaps, a little excessive. Talk to him about "moderation in all things." If you can once get him to the point of thinking that "religion is all very well up to a point," you can feel quite happy about his soul. A moderated religion is as good for us as no religion at all—and more amusing.

Another possibility is that of direct attack on his faith. When you have caused him to assume that the trough is permanent, can you not persuade him that "his religious phase" is just going to die away like all his previous phases? Of course there is no conceivable way of getting by reason from the proposition "I am losing interest in this" to the proposition "This is false." But, as I said before,[6] it is jargon, not reason, you must rely on. The mere word *phase* will very likely do the trick. I assume that the creature has been through several of them before—they all have—and that he always feels superior and patronising to the ones he has emerged from, not because he has really criticised them but simply because they are in the past.[7] (You keep him well fed on hazy ideas of Progress[8] and Development and the Historical Point of View,[9] I trust, and give him lots of modern Biographies to read? The people in them are always emerging from Phases, aren't they?)

6. At the start of "Letter 1" (p. 3).

7. In the first chapter of *The Allegory of Love*, Lewis explores a different perspective on phases: "Humanity does not pass through phases as a train passes through stations: being alive, it has the privilege of always moving yet never leaving anything behind. Whatever we have been, in some sort we are still."

8. "We all want progress," Lewis writes in *Mere Christianity*, book 1, chapter 5. "But progress means getting nearer to the place where you want to be. And if you have taken a wrong turning, then to go forward does not get you any nearer. If you are on the wrong road, progress means doing an about-turn and walking back to the right road; and in that case the man who turns back soonest is the most progressive man." In the essay "Evil and God" in *God in the Dock*, Lewis states, "There is no sense in talking of 'becoming better' if better means simply 'what we are becoming'—it is like congratulating yourself on reaching your destination and defining destination as 'the place you have reached.'"

9. This wry suggestion foreshadows the fuller explanation Screwtape presents about the Historical Point of View in "Letter 27" (p. 159).

You see the idea? Keep his mind off the plain antithesis between True and False. Nice shadowy expressions—"It was a phase"— "I've been through all that"—and don't forget the blessed word "Adolescent."[10]

Your affectionate uncle
Screwtape

10. Lewis represented this view through the character of Susan Pevensie, who dismissed any talk of Narnia as merely funny games the children once played. She was more "interested in nothing nowadays except nylons and lipstick and invitations" and being "grown-up." (*Last Battle*, chap. 12.)

Letter 10

My dear Wormwood,

First published in *The Guardian* on July 4, 1941.

I was delighted to hear from Triptweeze that your patient has made some very desirable new acquaintances and that you seem to have used this event in a really promising manner. I gather that the middle-aged married couple who called at his office are just the sort of people we want him to know—rich, smart, superficially intellectual, and brightly skeptical about everything in the world. I gather they are even vaguely pacifist, not on moral grounds but from an ingrained habit of belittling anything that concerns the great mass of their fellow men and from a dash of purely fashionable and literary communism. This is excellent. And you seem to have made good use of all his social, sexual, and intellectual vanity. Tell me more. Did

1. Lewis writes, "How ought we to behave in the presence of very bad people? I will limit this by changing 'very bad people' to 'very bad people who are powerful, prosperous and impenitent.' If they are outcasts, poor and miserable, whose wickedness obviously has not 'paid,' then every Christian knows the answer. . . . But I am inclined to think a Christian would be wise to avoid, where he decently can, any meeting with people who are bullies, lascivious, cruel, dishonest, spiteful and so forth. Not because we are 'too good' for them. In a sense, because we are not good enough. We are not good enough to cope with all the temptations, nor clever enough to cope with all the problems. . . . The temptation is to condone, to connive at; by our words, looks, and laughter, to 'consent.'" (*Reflections on the Psalms*, chap 7.)

2. "All mortals tend to turn into the thing they are pretending to be. This is elementary." Lewis reiterates this view positively in book 3, chapter 9 of *Mere Christianity*: "The rule for all of us is perfectly simple. Do not waste time bothering whether you 'love' your neighbour; act as if you did. As soon as we do this we find one of the great secrets. When you are behaving as if you loved someone, you will presently come to love him. If you injure someone you dislike, you will find yourself disliking him more. If you do him a good turn, you will find yourself disliking him less. There is, indeed, one exception. If you do him a good turn, not to please God and obey

he commit himself deeply? I don't mean in words. There is a subtle play of looks and tones and laughs by which a mortal can imply that he is of the same party as those to whom he is speaking.[1] That is the kind of betrayal you should specially encourage, because the man does not fully realize it himself; and by the time he does you will have made withdrawal difficult.

No doubt he must very soon realize that his own faith is in direct opposition to the assumptions on which all the conversation of his new friends is based. I don't think that matters much provided that you can persuade him to postpone any open acknowledgment of the fact, and this, with the aid of shame, pride, modesty, and vanity, will be easy to do. As long as the postponement lasts he will be in a false position. He will be silent when he ought to speak and laugh when he ought to be silent. He will assume, at first only by his manner, but presently by his words, all sorts of cynical and skeptical attitudes which are not really his. But if you play him well, they may become his. All mortals tend to turn into the thing they are pretending to be.[2] This is elementary. The real question is how to prepare for the Enemy's counterattack.

The first thing is to delay as long as possible the moment at which he realizes this new pleasure as a temptation. Since the Enemy's servants have been preaching about "the World" as one of the great standard temptations for two thousand years, this might seem difficult to do. But fortunately they have said very little about it for the last few decades. In modern Christian writings, though I see much (indeed more than I like) about Mammon,[3] I see few of the old warnings about Worldly Vanities, the Choice of Friends, and the Value of Time. All that, your patient would probably classify as "Puritanism"[4]—and may I remark in passing that the value we have given to that word is one of the really solid triumphs of the last hundred years?[5] By it we rescue annually thousands of humans from temperance, chastity, and sobriety of life.

Sooner or later, however, the real nature of his new friends must become clear to him, and then your tactics must depend on the patient's intelligence. If he is a big enough fool you can get him to realize the

the law of charity, but to show him what a fine forgiving chap you are, and to put him in your debt, and then sit down to wait for his 'gratitude,' you will probably be disappointed."

3. Mammon: money.

4. Puritans were a group of English Protestants of the sixteenth and seventeenth centuries who rebelled against the Church of England and Catholicism. "Puritanism" eventually became a pejorative expression for those Christians who seemed to have restrictive views on sexual morality and entertainments (theatre, recreation, games) and attempted to impose their practices on others. In the twentieth century virtually any prohibition or restraint of sexual activity on moral grounds was readily dismissed as mere "Puritanism."

5. In his essay "Edmund Spenser 1552–99," Lewis writes, "We must picture these Puritans as the very opposite of those who bear that name today: as young, fierce, progressive intellectuals, very fashionable and up-to-date. They were not teetotalers; bishops, not beer, were their special aversion." (*Medieval and Renaissance Literature.*)

character of the friends only while they are absent; their presence can be made to sweep away all criticism. If this succeeds, he can be induced to live, as I have known many humans live, for quite long periods, two parallel lives; he will not only appear to be, but actually be, a different man in each of the circles he frequents. Failing this, there is a subtler and more entertaining method. He can be made to take a positive pleasure in the perception that the two sides of his life are inconsistent. This is done by exploiting his vanity. He can be taught to enjoy kneeling beside the grocer on Sunday just because he remembers that the grocer could not possibly understand the urbane and mocking world which he inhabited on Saturday evening; and contrariwise, to enjoy the bawdy and blasphemy over the coffee with these admirable friends all the more because he is aware of a "deeper," "spiritual" world within him which they cannot understand. You see the idea—the worldly friends touch him on one side and the grocer on the other, and he is the complete, balanced, complex man who sees round them all. Thus, while being permanently treacherous to at least two sets of people, he will feel, instead of shame, a continual undercurrent of self-satisfaction. Finally, if all else fails, you can persuade him, in defiance of conscience, to continue the new acquaintance on the ground that he is, in some unspecified way, doing these people "good" by the mere fact of drinking their cocktails and laughing at their jokes, and that to cease to do so would be "priggish,"[6] "intolerant," and (of course) "Puritanical."

Meanwhile you will of course take the obvious precaution of seeing that this new development induces him to spend more than he can afford and to neglect his work and his mother. Her jealousy, and alarm, and his increasing evasiveness or rudeness, will be invaluable for the aggravation of the domestic tension,

Your affectionate uncle
Screwtape

6. Priggish: arrogant or smug, self-righteously correct. Eustace Scrubb, in Lewis's *The Voyage of the Dawn Treader,* could be considered a prig.

Letter 11

My dear Wormwood,

Everything is clearly going very well. I am specially glad to hear that the two new friends have now made him acquainted with their whole set.[1] All these, as I find from the record office, are thoroughly reliable people; steady, consistent scoffers and worldlings who without any spectacular crimes are progressing quietly and comfortably towards our Father's house. You speak of their being great laughers. I trust this does not mean that you are under the impression that laughter as such is always in our favour. The point is worth some attention.

I divide the causes of human laughter into Joy,[2] Fun, the Joke Proper, and Flippancy. You will see the first among friends and lovers reunited on the eve of a holiday.

First published in *The Guardian* on July 11, 1941.

1. Whole set: companions or clique.

2. Here "Joy" suggests a normal form of happiness. But another form of joy takes its place as a central theme in the works of Lewis, pervading much of his nonfiction, fiction, and poetic works. In chapter 1 of *Surprised By Joy,* he determines that "the central story of my life is about nothing else" and defines it as "that of an unsatisfied desire which is itself more desirable than any other satisfaction." He differentiates it from happiness and pleasure as being outside of "our power," but allows that it has one characteristic in common: "the fact that anyone who has experienced it will want it again." In chapter 5 of the same work, he describes joy as having "the stab, the pang, the inconsolable longing" and in chapter 11 he wonders "whether all pleasures are not substitutes for Joy." In his preface to his poem "Dymer," in *Narrative Poems,* he calls it *Sehnsucht,* a "romantic longing" that he'd experienced since the age of six. "Such longing is in itself the very reverse of wishful thinking: it is more like thoughtful wishing." Joy, though, is not an end in and of itself. It is a reminder of something greater and cries out, "Look! Look! What do I remind you of?" (*Surprised By Joy,* chap. 14). It is a signpost found in the woods by a lost party: "The whole party gathers round and stares. But when we have found the road and are passing signposts every few miles, we shall not stop and stare. They will encourage us and we shall be grateful to the authority that set them up" (*Surprised By Joy,* chap. 15). It is "spilled religion" (*Christian Reflections,* "Christianity and Culture"). It is "the door on which we have been knocking all our lives," one that will finally open and then "our lifelong nostalgia, our longing to be reunited with something in the universe from which we now feel cut off, to be on the inside of some door which we have always seen from the outside, is not mere neurotic fancy, but the truest index of our real situation. And to be at last summoned inside would be both glory and honour beyond all our merits and also the healing of that old ache" (*Weight of Glory*). It is "the serious business of heaven" (*Letters to Malcolm,* chap. 17) that Screwtape cannot comprehend, but Lewis describes its fulfillment in his final letter.

3. Friend and biographer Roger Lancelyn Green notes that Lewis himself did not use the word "bawdy" as meaning "dirty stories." In fact, he showed undisguised annoyance with stories "containing smut or that bordered upon the blasphemous." Lewis believed that bawdy "ought to be outrageous and extravagant, but it must not have anything cruel or pornographic

Among adults some pretext in the way of Jokes is usually provided, but the facility with which the smallest witticisms produce laughter at such a time shows that they are not the real cause. What that real cause is we do not know. Something like it is expressed in much of that detestable art which the humans call Music, and something like it occurs in Heaven—a meaningless acceleration in the rhythm of celestial experience, quite opaque to us. Laughter of this kind does us no good and should always be discouraged. Besides, the phenomenon is of itself disgusting and a direct insult to the realism, dignity, and austerity of Hell.

Fun is closely related to Joy—a sort of emotional froth arising from the play instinct. It is very little use to us. It can sometimes be used, of course, to divert humans from something else which the Enemy would like them to be feeling or doing: but in itself it has wholly undesirable tendencies; it promotes charity, courage, contentment, and many other evils.

The Joke Proper, which turns on sudden perception of incongruity, is a much more promising field. I am not thinking primarily of indecent or bawdy humour,[3] which, though much relied upon by second-rate tempters, is often disappointing in its results. The truth is that humans are pretty clearly divided on this matter into two classes. There are some to whom "no passion is as serious as lust" and for whom an indecent story ceases to produce lasciviousness precisely in so far as it becomes funny:[4] there are others in whom laughter and lust are excited at the same moment and by the same thing. The first sort joke about sex because it gives rise to many incongruities: the second cultivate incongruities because they afford a pretext for talking about sex. If your man is of the first type, bawdy humour will not help you—I shall never forget the hours which I wasted (hours to me of unbearable tedium) with one of my early patients in bars and smoking-rooms before I learned this rule. Find out which group the patient belongs to—and see that he does *not* find out.

The real use of Jokes or Humour is in quite a different direction, and it is specially promising among the English who take their "sense of humour" so seriously that a deficiency in this sense is almost the only deficiency at which they feel shame.

about it." (*At Breakfast,* chap. 20, "In the Evening.")

4. In his book *Surprised By Laughter: The Comic World of C. S. Lewis,* scholar Terry Lindvall writes, "At the wrong moment, Lewis writes, laughter is 'fatal to sensuality'" (p. 328). He then quotes Lewis from *English Literature in the Sixteenth Century,* in which Lewis observes that "Byron and Ovid keep their sensuality tolerable (when they do) by being comic and ironical and thus write a wholly different sort of poetry" (p. 488).

Humour is for them the all-consoling and (mark this) the all-excusing, grace of life. Hence it is invaluable as a means of destroying shame. If a man simply lets others pay for him, he is "mean"; if he boasts of it in a jocular manner and twits his fellows with having been scored off,[5] he is no longer "mean" but a comical fellow. Mere cowardice is shameful; cowardice boasted of with humorous exaggerations and grotesque gestures can be passed off as funny. Cruelty is shameful—unless the cruel man can represent it as a practical joke. A thousand bawdy, or even blasphemous, jokes do not help towards a man's damnation so much as his discovery that almost anything he wants to do can be done, not only without the disapproval but with the admiration of his fellows, if only it can get itself treated as a Joke. And this temptation can be almost entirely hidden from your patient by that English seriousness about Humour. Any suggestion that there might be too much of it can be represented to him as "Puritanical" or as betraying a "lack of humour."

But flippancy[6] is the best of all. In the first place it is very economical. Only a clever human can make a real Joke about virtue, or indeed about anything else; any of them can be trained to talk *as if* virtue were funny. Among flippant people the Joke is always assumed to have been made. No one actually makes it; but every serious subject is discussed in a manner which implies that they have already found a ridiculous side to it. If prolonged, the habit of Flippancy builds up around a man the finest armour-plating against the Enemy that I know, and it is quite free from the dangers inherent in the other sources of laughter. It is a thousand miles away from joy: it deadens, instead of sharpening, the intellect; and it excites no affection between those who practice it,

Your affectionate uncle
Screwtape

Letter 12

My dear Wormwood,

First published in *The Guardian* on July 18, 1941.

Obviously you are making excellent progress. My only fear is lest in attempting to hurry the patient you awaken him to a sense of his real position. For you and I, who see that position as it really is, must never forget how totally different it ought to appear to him. We know that we have introduced a change of direction in his course which is already carrying him out of his orbit around the Enemy; but he must be made to imagine that all the choices which have effected this change of course are trivial and revocable. He must not be allowed to suspect that he is now, however slowly, heading right away from the sun on a line which will carry him into the cold and dark of utmost space.

For this reason I am almost glad to hear that he is still a churchgoer and a communicant. I know there are dangers in this; but anything is better than that he should realize the break he has made with the first months of his Christian life. As long as he retains externally the habits of a Christian he can still be made to think of himself as one who has adopted a few new friends and amusements but whose spiritual state is much the same as it was six weeks ago. And while he thinks that, we do not have to contend with the explicit repentance of a definite, fully recognised, sin, but only with his vague, though uneasy, feeling that he hasn't been doing very well lately.

This dim uneasiness needs careful handling. If it gets too strong it may wake him up and spoil the whole game. On the other hand, if you suppress it entirely—which, by the by, the Enemy will probably not allow you to do—we lose an element in the situation which can be turned to good account. If such a feeling is allowed to live, but not allowed to become irresistible and flower into real repentance, it has one invaluable tendency. It increases the patient's reluctance to think about the Enemy. All humans at nearly all times have some such reluctance; but when thinking of Him involves facing and intensifying a whole vague cloud of half-conscious guilt, this reluctance is increased tenfold.[1] They hate every idea that suggests Him, just as men in financial embarrassment hate the very sight of a pass-book.[2] In this state your patient will not omit, but he will increasingly dislike, his religious duties. He will think about them as little as he feels he decently can beforehand, and forget them as soon as possible when they are over. A few weeks ago you had to *tempt* him to unreality and inattention in his prayers: but now you will find him opening his arms to you and almost begging you to distract his purpose and benumb his heart. He will *want* his prayers to be unreal, for he will dread nothing so much as effective contact with the Enemy. His aim will be to let sleeping worms lie.[3]

As this condition becomes more fully established, you will be gradually freed from the tiresome business of providing Pleasures as temptations. As the uneasiness and his reluctance to face it cut him off more and more from all real happiness, and as habit renders the pleasures of vanity and excitement and

1. "What the devil loves is that vague cloud of unspecified guilt or feeling or unspecified virtue by which he lures us into despair or presumption. 'Details, please?' is the answer." (Letter dated July 21, 1958, in *Letters to an American Lady*.)

2. Pass-book: bank book.

3. A hellish equivalent to "let sleeping dogs lie."

4. A variation on a collect from the Book of Common Prayer: "O God, the protector of all that trust in Thee, without whom nothing is strong, nothing is holy: increase and multiply upon us Thy mercy."

flippancy at once less pleasant and harder to forgo (for that is what habit fortunately does to a pleasure) you will find that anything or nothing is sufficient to attract his wandering attention. You no longer need a good book, which he really likes, to keep him from his prayers or his work or his sleep; a column of advertisements in yesterday's paper will do. You can make him waste his time not only in conversation he enjoys with people whom he likes, but in conversations with those he cares nothing about on subjects that bore him. You can make him do nothing at all for long periods.

You can keep him up late at night, not roistering, but staring at a dead fire in a cold room. All the healthy and outgoing activities which we want him to avoid can be inhibited and *nothing* given in return, so that at last he may say, as one of my own patients said on his arrival down here, "I now see that I spent most of my life in doing *neither* what I ought nor what I liked." The Christians describe the Enemy as one "without whom Nothing is strong."[4] And Nothing is very strong: strong enough to steal away a man's best years not in sweet sins but in a dreary flickering of the mind over it knows not what and knows not why, in the gratification of curiosities so feeble that the man is only half aware of them, in drumming of fingers and kicking of heels, in whistling tunes that he does not like, or in the long, dim labyrinth of reveries that have not even lust or ambition to give them a relish, but which, once chance association has started them, the creature is too weak and fuddled to shake off.

You will say that these are very small sins; and doubtless, like all young tempters, you are anxious to be able to report spectacular wickedness. But do remember, the only thing that matters is the extent to which you separate the man from the Enemy. It does not matter how small the sins are provided that their cumulative effect is to edge the man away from the Light and out into the Nothing. Murder is no better than cards if cards can do the trick.[5] Indeed the safest road to Hell is the gradual one—the gentle slope, soft underfoot, without sudden turnings, without milestones, without signposts,

Your affectionate uncle
Screwtape

[5] "The sins of the flesh are bad, but they are the least bad of all sins. All the worst pleasures are purely spiritual: the pleasure of putting other people in the wrong, of bossing and patronizing and spoiling sport, and back-biting; the pleasures of power, of hatred. For there are two things inside me, competing with the human self which I must try to become. They are the Animal self, and the Diabolical self. The Diabolical self is the worse of the two. That is why a cold, self-righteous prig who goes regularly to church may be far nearer to hell than a prostitute. But, of course, it is better to be neither." (*Mere Christianity*, bk. 3, chap. 5.)

Letter 13

My dear Wormwood,

t seems to me that you take a great many pages to tell a very simple story. The long and the short of it is that you have let the man slip through your fingers. The situation is very grave, and I really see no reason why I should try to shield you from the consequences of your inefficiency. A repentance and renewal of what the other side call "grace" on the scale which you describe is a defeat of the first order. It amounts to a second conversion—and probably on a deeper level than the first.

As you ought to have known, the asphyxiating cloud[1] which prevented your attacking the patient on his walk back from the old mill, is a well-known phenomenon. It is the Enemy's most barbarous weapon, and generally appears when He is directly

First published in *The Guardian* on July 25, 1941.

1. A cloud in the Bible was often the symbol of God's activity and the Holy Spirit. A bow was set in a cloud as a token of the covenant between God and Noah (Genesis 9); a cloud led the children of Israel through the wilderness (Exodus 13:20–22); a cloud covered the tent and tabernacle (Exodus 40) and other holy places (I Kings 8, Ezekiel 10); a cloud covered Jesus and three disciples on the Mount of Transfiguration (Mark 9); a cloud appeared at the commissioning of the seventy elders (Numbers 11) and at Pentecost (Acts 2). Lewis allows that what appeared radiant and glorious to those participants was asphyxiating to the demonic world. And, as a soldier in World War I, Lewis would well remember the use of gases and smoke to create an asphyxiating cloud to choke and confuse the enemy.

2. The pleasure of the tea in this context is an interesting contrast to the tea twisted by the mother in "Letter 12" (p. 69).

3. Lewis was an avid walker, often taking long "rambles" through the English countryside alone or with friends, stopping at pubs or teahouses along the way.

4. In chapter 6 of *The Problem of Pain,* Lewis writes, "Pain insists upon being attended to. God whispers to us in our pleasures, speaks in our conscience, but shouts in our pains: it is His megaphone to rouse a deaf world."

5. Childe Harold was the protagonist in George Byron's (1788–1824) poem "Childe Harold's Pilgrimage: A Romaunt" (1812–1818), a poem in four cantos. Mirroring Lord Byron's own life, the hero becomes disillusioned with pleasure and self-indulgence and goes to faraway lands to find distraction.

6. Werther was the main character in *The Sorrows of Young Werther,* the first published novel by Johann Wolfgang von Goethe (1749–1832). Written as a series of letters from Werther to a friend, the novel chronicles the emotional and romantic misfortunes of the protagonist. The novel later influenced the Romantic literary movement.

present to the patient under certain modes not yet fully classified. Some humans are permanently surrounded by it and therefore inaccessible to us.

And now for your blunders. On your own showing you first of all allowed the patient to read a book he really enjoyed, because he enjoyed it and not in order to make clever remarks about it to his new friends. In the second place, you allowed him to walk down to the old mill and have tea[2] there—a walk through country he really likes, and taken alone.[3] In other words you allowed him two real positive Pleasures. Were you so ignorant as not to see the danger of this? The characteristic of Pains and Pleasures is that they are unmistakably real, and therefore, as far as they go, give the man who feels them a touchstone of reality.[4] Thus if you had been trying to damn your man by the Romantic method—by making him a kind of Childe Harold[5] or Werther[6] submerged in self-pity for imaginary distresses—you would try to protect him at all costs from any real pain; because, of course, five minutes' genuine toothache would reveal the romantic sorrows for the nonsense they were and unmask your whole stratagem. But you were trying to damn your patient by the World, that is by palming off vanity, bustle, irony, and expensive tedium as pleasures. How can you have failed to see that a *real* pleasure was the last thing you ought to have let him meet? Didn't you foresee that it would just kill by contrast all the trumpery which you have been so laboriously teaching him to value? And that the sort of pleasure which the book and the walk gave him was the most dangerous of all? That it would peel off from his sensibility the kind of crust you have been forming on it, and make him feel that he was coming home, recovering himself? As a preliminary to detaching him from the Enemy, you wanted to detach him from himself, and had made some progress in doing so. Now, all that is undone.

Of course I know that the Enemy also wants to detach men from themselves, but in a different way. Remember always, that He really likes the little vermin, and sets an absurd value on the distinctness of every one of them. When He talks of their losing their selves, He only means abandoning the clamour of self-will; once they have done that, He really gives them back all their personality, and boasts (I am afraid, sincerely) that when they are wholly His they will be more themselves than ever. Hence, while He is delighted to see them sacrificing even their innocent wills to His, He hates to see them drifting away from their own nature for any other reason. And we should always encourage them to do so. The deepest likings and impulses of any man are the raw material, the starting-point, with which the Enemy has furnished him. To get him away from those is therefore always a point gained; even in things indifferent it is always desirable to substitute the standards of the World, or convention, or fashion, for a human's own real likings and dislikings. I myself would carry this very far. I would make it a rule to eradicate from my patient any strong personal taste which is not actually a sin, even if it is something quite trivial such as a fondness for county cricket or collecting stamps or drinking cocoa. Such things, I grant you, have nothing of virtue in them; but there is a sort of innocence and humility and self-forgetfulness about them which I distrust. The man who truly and disinterestedly enjoys any one thing in the world, for its own sake, and without caring two-pence[7] what other people say about it, is by that very fact fore-armed against some of our subtlest modes of attack. You should always try to make the patient abandon the people or food or books he really likes in favour of the "best" people, the "right" food, the "important" books. I have known a human defended from strong temptations to social ambition by a still stronger taste for tripe and onions.[8]

It remains to consider how we can retrieve this disaster. The great thing is to prevent his doing anything. As long as he does not convert it into action, it does not matter how much he thinks about this new repentance. Let the little brute wallow in it. Let him, if he has any bent that way, write a book about it; that is often an excellent way of sterilising the seeds which the Enemy plants in a human soul. Let him do anything but act. No amount of piety in his imagination and affections will harm us if we can keep it out of his will. As one of the humans has said, active habits are strengthened by repetition but passive ones are weakened.[9] The more often he feels

7. Two-pence (tuppence) was the expression used for two pennies in British coinage. In this context, it means he couldn't care less.

8. A dish from northern England involving the edible portion of the stomach lining of a cow or sheep, mixed with onions.

9. Likely a quote from Belfast-born poet, philosopher, and scientist Joseph John Murphy (1827–1894), from his *Habit and Intelligence, In Their Connection with the Laws of Matter and Force*. In chapter 15 he wrote, "The habits of the species or genus are most tenacious, those of the individual often the most prominent. . . . The fact that active habits are strengthened, while passive impressions are weakened, by repetition, is due in both cases to the law of habit; for, in the latter, the organism acquires the habit of not responding to the impression. As an example, two men hear the same loud bell in the morning; it calls the one to work, as he is accustomed to listen to it, and so it always wakes him; the other has to rise an hour later, he is accustomed to disregard it, and so it soon ceases to have any effect upon him. Habit has produced in these two cases exactly opposite results."

without acting, the less he will be able ever to act, and, in the long run, the less he will be able to feel,

Your affectionate uncle
Screwtape

Letter 14

My dear Wormwood,

The most alarming thing in your last account of the patient is that he is making none of those confident resolutions which marked his original conversion. No more lavish promises of perpetual virtue, I gather; not even the expectation of an endowment of "grace" for life, but only a hope for the daily and hourly pittance to meet the daily and hourly temptation! This is very bad.

I see only one thing to do at the moment. Your patient has become humble; have you drawn his attention to the fact? All virtues are less formidable to us once the man is aware that he has them, but this is specially true of humility.[1] Catch him at the moment when he is really poor in spirit[2] and smuggle into his mind the gratifying reflection,

First published in *The Guardian* on August 1, 1941.

1. "Do not imagine that if you meet a really humble man he will be what most people call 'humble' nowadays: he will not be a sort of greasy, smarmy person, who is always telling you that, of course, he is nobody. Probably all you will think about him is that he seemed a cheerful, intelligent chap who took a real interest in what *you* said to *him*. . . . He will not be thinking about humility: he will not be thinking about himself at all." (*Mere Christianity*, bk. 3, chap. 8.)

2. From the Gospel of Matthew 5:3. "Blessed are the poor in spirit for theirs is the Kingdom of Heaven." "Poor in Spirit" is traditionally interpreted as humility.

"By Jove![3] I'm being humble," and almost immediately pride—pride at his own humility—will appear.[4] If he awakes to the danger and tries to smother this new form of pride, make him proud of his attempt—and so on, through as many stages as you please. But don't try this too long, for fear you awake his sense of humour and proportion, in which case he will merely laugh at you and go to bed.

But there are other profitable ways of fixing his attention on the virtue of Humility. By this virtue, as by all the others, our Enemy wants to turn the man's attention away from self to Him, and to the man's neighbours. All the abjection[5] and self-hatred are designed, in the long run, solely for this end; unless they attain this end they do us little harm; and they may even do us good if they keep the man concerned with himself, and, above all, if self-contempt can be made the starting-point for contempt of other selves, and thus for gloom, cynicism, and cruelty.

You must therefore conceal from the patient the true end of Humility. Let him think of it not as self-forgetfulness but as a certain kind of opinion (namely, a low opinion) of his own talents and character.

Some talents, I gather, he really has. Fix in his mind the idea that humility consists in trying to believe those talents to be less valuable than he believes them to be. No doubt they *are* in fact less valuable than he believes, but that is not the point. The great thing is to make him value an opinion for some quality other than truth, thus introducing an element of dishonesty and make-believe into the heart of what otherwise threatens to become a virtue. By this method thousands of humans have been brought to think that humility means pretty women trying to believe they are ugly and clever men trying to believe they are fools. And since what they are trying to believe may, in some cases, be manifest nonsense, they cannot succeed in believing it and we have the chance of keeping their minds endlessly revolving on themselves in an effort to achieve the impossible. To anticipate the Enemy's strategy, we must consider His aims. The Enemy wants to bring the man to a state of mind in which he could design the best cathedral in the world, and know it to be the best, and rejoice in the fact, without being any more (or less) or otherwise glad at having done it than he would be if it had been done by another. The Enemy wants him, in the end, to be so free from any bias in his own favour that he can rejoice in his own talents as frankly and gratefully as in his neighbour's talents—or in a sunrise, an elephant, or a waterfall. He wants each man, in the long run, to be able to recognise all creatures (even himself) as glorious and excellent things. He wants to kill their animal self-love as soon as possible; but it is His long-term policy, I fear, to restore to them a new kind of self-love—a charity and gratitude for all selves, including their own; when they have really learned to love their neighbours as themselves, they will be allowed to love themselves as their neighbours. For we must never forget what is the most repellent and inexplicable trait in our Enemy; He *really* loves the hairless bipeds He has created and always gives back to them with His right hand what He has taken away with His left.

His whole effort, therefore, will be to get the man's mind off the subject of his own value altogether. He would rather the man thought himself a great architect or a great poet and then forgot about it, than that he should spend much time and pains trying to think himself a bad one. Your efforts to instill either vainglory or false modesty into the patient will therefore be met from the Enemy's side with the obvious reminder that a man is not usually called upon to have an opinion of his own talents at all, since he can very well go on improving them to the best of his ability without deciding on his own precise niche in the temple of Fame. You must try to exclude this reminder from the patient's consciousness at all costs. The Enemy will also try to render real in the patient's mind a doctrine which they all profess but find it difficult to bring home to their feelings—the doctrine that they did not create themselves, that their talents were given them, and that they might as well be proud of the colour of their hair. But always and by all methods the Enemy's aim will be to get the patient's mind off such questions, and yours will be to fix it on them. Even of his sins the Enemy does not want him to think too much: once they are repented, the sooner the man turns his attention outward, the better the Enemy is pleased,

Your affectionate uncle
Screwtape

Letter 15

My dear Wormwood,

I had noticed, of course, that the humans were having a lull in their European war—what they naïvely call "*The War!*"—and am not surprised that there is a corresponding lull in the patient's anxieties. Do we want to encourage this, or to keep him worried? Tortured fear and stupid confidence are both desirable states of mind. Our choice between them raises important questions.

The humans live in time but our Enemy destines them to eternity. He therefore, I believe, wants them to attend chiefly to two things, to eternity itself, and to that point of time which they call the Present. For the Present is the point at which time touches eternity.[1] Of the present moment, and of it only, humans have an experience

First published in *The Guardian* on August 8, 1941. It is worth noting that two days before this C. S. Lewis offered the first of four BBC broadcast "talks." The series, which broadcast on Wednesdays at 7:45 P.M. and would last for fifteen minutes, was called "Right and Wrong." The subtitle was "A Clue to the Meaning of the Universe?" The subject of the first talk was common decency. The content of these broadcasts, and subsequent talks the following year, later became *Mere Christianity*.

1. "Where, except in the present, can the Eternal be met?" (*Christian Reflections*, "Historicism.")

analogous to the experience which our Enemy has of reality as a whole; in it alone freedom and actuality are offered them. He would therefore have them continually concerned either with eternity (which means being concerned with Him) or with the Present—either meditating on their eternal union with, or separation from, Himself, or else obeying the present voice of conscience, bearing the present cross, receiving the present grace, giving thanks for the present pleasure.

Our business is to get them away from the eternal, and from the Present. With this in view, we sometimes tempt a human (say a widow or a scholar) to live in the Past. But this is of limited value, for they have some real knowledge of the past and it has a determinate nature and, to that extent, resembles eternity. It is far better to make them live in the Future. Biological necessity makes all their passions point in that direction already, so that thought about the Future inflames hope and fear. Also, it is unknown to them, so that in making them think about it we make them think of unrealities. In a word, the Future is, of all things, the thing *least like* eternity. It is the most completely temporal part of time—for the Past is frozen and no longer flows, and the Present is all lit up with eternal rays. Hence the encouragement we have given to all those schemes of thought such as Creative Evolution,[2] Scientific Humanism,[3] or Communism,[4] which fix men's affections on the Future, on the very core of temporality. Hence nearly all vices are rooted in the future. Gratitude looks to the past and love to the present; fear, avarice, lust, and ambition look ahead. Do not think lust an exception. When the present pleasure arrives, the sin (which alone interests us) is already over. The pleasure is just the part of the process which we regret and would exclude if we could do so without losing the sin; it is the part contributed by the Enemy, and therefore experienced in a Present. The sin, which is our contribution, looked forward.

To be sure, the Enemy wants men to think of the Future too—just so much as is necessary for *now* planning the acts of justice or charity which will probably be their duty tomorrow. The duty of planning the morrow's work is *today's* duty; though its material is borrowed from the future, the

2. Creative evolution was a concept developed by the French philosopher Henri-Louis Bergson (1858–1941). See note 1 in "Letter 7" (p. 40).

3. Simplistically stated, scientific humanism, a variation of secular humanism, advocated that humankind's full potential could be achieved only through strictly human effort, knowledge, and understanding, not through religious values or any relationship with a supernatural God or force. There is no single author of this view, but its greatest popularity emerged in the nineteenth and twentieth centuries.

4. Communism is an ideology that strives to establish a classless and moneyless society based on common ownership of the production of all goods and services.

duty, like all duties, is in the Present. This is not straw splitting. He does not want men to give the Future their hearts, to place their treasure in it. We do. His ideal is a man who, having worked all day for the good of posterity (if that is his vocation), washes his mind of the whole subject, commits the issue to Heaven, and returns at once to the patience or gratitude demanded by the moment that is passing over him. But we want a man hag-ridden by the Future—haunted by visions of an imminent heaven or hell upon earth—ready to break the Enemy's commands in the present if by so doing we make him think he can attain the one or avert the other—dependent for his faith on the success or failure of schemes whose end he will not live to see. We want a whole race perpetually in pursuit of the rainbow's end, never honest, nor kind, nor happy *now*, but always using as mere fuel wherewith to heap the altar of the future every real gift which is offered them in the Present.

It follows then, in general, and other things being equal, that it is better for your patient to be filled with anxiety or hope (it doesn't much matter which) about this war than for him to be living in the present. But the phrase "living in the present" is ambiguous. It may describe a process which is really just as much concerned with the Future as anxiety itself. Your man may be untroubled about the Future, not because he is concerned with the Present, but because he has persuaded himself that the Future is going to be agreeable. As long as that is the real course of his tranquility, his tranquility will do us good, because it is only piling up more disappointment, and therefore more impatience, for him when his false hopes are dashed. If, on the other hand, he is aware that horrors may be in store for him and is praying for the virtues, wherewith to meet them, and meanwhile concerning himself with the Present because there, and there alone, all duty, all grace, all knowledge, and all pleasure dwell, his state is very undesirable and should be attacked at once. Here again, our Philological[5] Arm has done good work; try the word "complacency" on him. But, of course, it is most likely that he is "living in the Present" for none of these reasons but simply because his health is good and he is enjoying his work. The phenomenon would then be merely natural.

5. Philology is the study of language in historical texts.

All the same, I should break it up if I were you. No natural phenomenon is really in our favour. And anyway, why *should* the creature be happy?

Your affectionate uncle
Screwtape

Letter 16

My dear Wormwood,

ou mentioned casually in your last letter that the patient has continued to attend one church, and one only, since he was converted, and that he is not wholly pleased with it. May I ask what you are about? Why have I no report on the causes of his fidelity to the parish[1] church? Do you realize that unless it is due to indifference it is a very bad thing? Surely you know that if a man can't be cured of churchgoing, the next best thing is to send him all over the neighbourhood looking for the church that "suits" him until he becomes a taster or connoisseur of churches.

The reasons are obvious. In the first place the parochial organisation[2] should always be attacked, because, being a unity of place and not of likings, it brings people of different classes and psychology together

First published in *The Guardian* on August 15, 1941.

1. In the Anglican, Catholic, and other traditional churches, a "parish" is the local division within a broader territory, a "diocese," which has its own church and member of the clergy. It is often based on geographical areas. So, in this case Screwtape is referring to the "patient's" local church nearest to his house.

2. The organization that runs or manages a parish.

3. "The New Testament does not envisage solitary religion; some kind of regular assembly for worship and instruction is everywhere taken for granted in the Epistles. So we must be regular practising members of the Church . . . For the Church is not a human society of people united by their natural affinities but the Body of Christ, in which all members, however different, (and He rejoices in their differences and by no means wishes to iron them out) must share the common life, complementing and helping one another precisely by their differences." (Letter dated December 7, 1950, in *Collected Letters III*.)

4. The "congregational principle" emerged in many churches and denominations around the time of the Protestant Reformation. The view espoused individual church governance based on the common beliefs of the congregation and eliminated the diocesan-parish structure.

in the kind of unity the Enemy desires.[3] The congregational principle,[4] on the other hand, makes each church into a kind of club, and finally, if all goes well, into a coterie or faction. In the second place, the search for a "suitable" church makes the man a critic where the Enemy wants him to be a pupil. What He wants of the layman in church is an attitude which may, indeed, be critical in the sense of rejecting what is false or unhelpful, but which is wholly uncritical in the sense that it does not appraise—does not waste time in thinking about what it rejects, but lays itself open in uncommenting, humble receptivity to any nourishment that is going. (You see how groveling, how unspiritual, how irredeemably vulgar He is!) This attitude, especially during sermons, creates the condition (most hostile to our whole policy) in which platitudes can become really audible to a human soul. There is hardly any sermon, or any book, which may not be dangerous to us if it is received in this temper. So pray bestir yourself and send this fool the round of the neighbouring churches as soon as possible. Your record up to date has not given us much satisfaction.

The two churches nearest to him, I have looked up in the office. Both have certain claims. At the first of these the Vicar is a man who has been so long engaged in watering down the faith to make it easier for a supposedly incredulous and hard-headed congregation that it is now he who shocks his parishioners with his unbelief, not *vice versa*. He has undermined many a soul's Christianity. His conduct of the services is also admirable. In order to spare the laity all "difficulties" he has deserted both the lectionary[5] and the appointed psalms and now, without noticing it, revolves endlessly round the little treadmill of his fifteen favourite psalms and twenty favourite lessons. We are thus safe from the danger that any truth not already familiar to him and to his flock should ever reach them through Scripture. But perhaps your patient is not quite silly enough for this church—or not yet?

At the other church we have Fr. Spike. The humans are often puzzled to understand the range of his opinions—why he is one day almost a Communist and the next not far from some kind of theocratic Fascism[6]— one day a scholastic, and the next prepared to deny human reason altogether—one day

5. A lectionary includes a denomination's prescribed scripture readings for all of its churches throughout a church calendar year.

6. Fascism is a political movement that promotes a centralized dictatorial government that holds control over all aspects of enterprise and culture, based on an extreme sense of nationalism. A theocratic version would put God in place of government.

7. Derived from various verses of scripture about God's interaction with human governments, "under judgment" suggests that God will thwart, diminish, or destroy governments if they do not serve his purposes or they actively work against him.

8. Jacques Maritain (1882–1973) was a French Catholic philosopher and essayist.

9. Party churches are those churches that have intentionally or unintentionally built themselves up around certain practices of worship or the faith.

immersed in politics, and, the day after, declaring that all states of this world are *equally* "under judgment."[7] We, of course, see the connecting link, which is Hatred. The man cannot bring himself to preach anything which is not calculated to shock, grieve, puzzle, or humiliate his parents and their friends. A sermon which such people could accept would be to him as insipid as a poem which they could scan. There is also a promising streak of dishonesty in him; we are teaching him to say "The teaching of the Church is" when he really means "I'm almost sure I read recently in Maritain[8] or someone of that sort." But I must warn you that he has one fatal defect: he really believes. And this may yet mar all.

But there is one good point which both these churches have in common—they are both party churches.[9] I think I warned you before that if your patient can't be kept out of the Church, he ought at least to be violently attached to some party within it. I don't mean on really doctrinal issues; about those, the more lukewarm he is the better. And it isn't the doctrines on which we chiefly depend for producing malice. The real fun is working up hatred between those who *say* "mass" and those who *say* "holy communion" when neither party could possibly state the difference between, say, Hooker's[10] doctrine and Thomas Aquinas',[11] in any form which would hold water for five minutes. And all the purely indifferent things—candles and clothes and what not—are an admirable ground for our activities. We have quite removed from men's minds what that pestilent fellow Paul[12] used to teach about food and other unessentials—namely, that the human without scruples should always give in to the human with scruples.[13] You would think they could not fail to see the application. You would expect to find the "low" churchman genuflecting and crossing himself lest the weak conscience of his "high" brother should be moved to irreverence, and the "high" one refraining from these exercises lest he should betray his "low" brother into idolatry. And so it would have been but for our ceaseless labour. Without that the variety of usage within the Church of England might have become a positive hotbed of charity and humility,

Your affectionate uncle
Screwtape

10. Richard Hooker (1564–1600) was a prominent Anglican theologian and priest who significantly influenced the theological underpinnings of the Church of England—and Anglicanism—in its infancy.

11. Thomas Aquinas (1225–1274) was an Italian Catholic priest and one of the most important philosophers and theologians of the medieval era.

12. The Apostle Paul.

13. In chapter 8 of his first letter to the church in Corinth, the Apostle Paul addressed the issue of Christians eating food that had been sacrificed to idols. While he argued that it is permissible, he also encouraged those who do it to be mindful of those who are "weak" in the faith and might find the practice to be a "stumbling block" to their spiritual growth.

Letter 17

My dear Wormwood,

First published in *The Guardian* on August 22, 1941.

The contemptuous way in which you spoke of gluttony as a means of catching souls, in your last letter, only shows your ignorance. One of the great achievements of the last hundred years has been to deaden the human conscience on that subject, so that by now you will hardly find a sermon preached or a conscience troubled about it in the whole length and breadth of Europe. This has largely been effected by concentrating all our efforts on gluttony of Delicacy, not gluttony of Excess. Your patient's mother, as I learn from the dossier and you might have learned from Glubose, is a good example. She would be astonished—one day, I hope, *will* be—to learn that her whole life is enslaved to this kind of sensuality, which is quite concealed

• 99

from her by the fact that the quantities involved are small. But what do quantities matter, provided we can use a human belly and palate to produce querulousness,[1] impatience, uncharitableness, and self-concern? Glubose has this old woman well in hand. She is a positive terror to hostesses and servants. She is always turning from what has been offered her to say with a demure little sigh and a smile "Oh please, please . . . *all* I want is a cup of tea, weak but not too weak, and the teeniest weeniest bit of really crisp toast." You see? Because what she wants is smaller and less costly than what has been set before her, she never recognises as gluttony her determination to get what she wants, however troublesome it may be to others. At the very moment of indulging her appetite she believes that she is practising temperance. In a crowded restaurant she gives a little scream at the plate which some overworked waitress has set before her and says, "Oh, that's far, far too much! Take it away and bring me about a quarter of it." If challenged, she would say she was doing this to avoid waste; in reality she does it because the particular shade of delicacy to which we have enslaved her is offended by the sight of more food than she happens to want.

The real value of the quiet, unobtrusive work which Glubose has been doing for years on this old woman can be gauged by the way in which her belly now dominates her whole life. The woman is in what may be called the "All-I-want" state of mind. *All* she wants is a cup of tea properly made, or an egg properly boiled, or a slice of bread properly toasted. But she never finds any servant or any friend who can do these simple things "properly"—because her "properly" conceals an insatiable demand for the exact, and almost impossible, palatal pleasures which she imagines she remembers from the past; a past described by her as "the days when you could get good servants" but known to us as the days when her senses were more easily pleased and she had pleasures of other kinds which made her less dependent on those of the table. Meanwhile, the daily disappointment produces daily ill temper: cooks give notice and friendships are cooled. If ever the Enemy introduces into her mind a faint suspicion that she is too interested in food, Glubose counters it by suggesting to her that she doesn't mind

2. In *The Four Loves,* chapter 3, Lewis mentions a "Mrs. Fidget, who died a few months ago" and how "her family has brightened up. The drawn look has gone from her husband's face; he begins to be able to laugh." The son, the daughter, even the dog, seem to have blossomed. Why? "Mrs. Fidget very often said that she lived for her family. And it was not untrue." She did the laundry—badly—though the family "begged her not to do it." In spite of her family's insistence that they liked cold meals, "there was always a hot lunch for anyone who was at home and always a hot meal at night. . . . It made no difference. She was living for her family." She was an amateur dressmaker and knitter, who made you feel heartless if you didn't wear what she'd made. "For Mrs. Fidget, as she so often said, would 'work her fingers to the bone' for her family. They couldn't stop her. Nor could they—being decent people—quite sit still and watch her do it. Indeed they were always having to help. That is, they did things for her to help her to do things for them which they didn't want done. . . . The Vicar says Mrs. Fidget is now at rest. Let us hope she is. What's quite certain is that her family are."

3. *Sole Colbert:* a fish dish named after a French minister in the court of Louis XIV, involving sole made with flour, eggs, breadcrumbs, then fried and infused with melted tarragon butter. Popularly served in upper-class British restaurants and hotels.

what she eats herself but "does like to have things nice for her boy." In fact, of course, her greed has been one of the chief sources of his domestic discomfort for many years.[2]

Now your patient is his mother's son. While working your hardest, quite rightly, on other fronts, you must not neglect a little quiet infiltration in respect of gluttony. Being a male, he is not so likely to be caught by the "*All* I want" camouflage. Males are best turned into gluttons with the help of their vanity. They ought to be made to think themselves very knowing about food, to pique themselves on having found the only restaurant in the town where steaks are really "properly" cooked. What begins as vanity can then be gradually turned into habit. But, however you approach it, the great thing is to bring him into the state in which the denial of any one indulgence—it matters not which, champagne or tea, *sole colbert*[3] or cigarettes—"puts him out," for then his charity, justice, and obedience are all at your mercy.

Mere excess in food is much less valuable than delicacy. Its chief use is as a kind of artillery preparation for attacks on chastity.

On that, as on every other subject, keep your man in a condition of false spirituality. Never let him notice the medical aspect. Keep him wondering what pride or lack of faith has delivered him into your hands when a simple enquiry into what he has been eating or drinking for the last twenty-four hours would show him whence your ammunition comes and thus enable him by a very little abstinence to imperil your lines of communication. If he *must* think of the medical side of chastity, feed him the grand lie which we have made the English humans believe, that physical exercise in excess and consequent fatigue are specially favourable to this virtue. How they can believe this, in face of the notorious lustfulness of sailors and soldiers, may well be asked. But we used the schoolmasters to put the story about—men who were really interested in chastity as an excuse for games and therefore recommended games as an aid to chastity. But this whole business is too large to deal with at the tail end of a letter,

Your affectionate uncle
Screwtape

Letter 18

My dear Wormwood,

Even under Slubgob you must have learned at college the routine technique of sexual temptation, and since, for us spirits, this whole subject is one of considerable tedium (though necessary as part of our training) I will pass it over. But on the larger issues involved I think you have a good deal to learn.

The Enemy's demand on humans takes the form of a dilemma; *either* complete abstinence or unmitigated monogamy. Ever since our Father's first great victory,[1] we have rendered the former very difficult to them. The latter, for the last few centuries, we have been closing up as a way of escape. We have done this through the poets and novelists by persuading the humans that a curious, and usually short-lived, experience

First published in *The Guardian* on August 29, 1941.

1. Presumably the Fall of Humanity as depicted in Genesis, chapter 3.

2. Lewis writes in book 3, chapter 6, of *Mere Christianity,* "Being in love is a good thing, but it is not the best thing. There are many things below it, but there are also things above it. You cannot make it the basis of a whole life. It is a noble feeling, but it is still a feeling.... But, of course, ceasing to be 'in love' need not mean ceasing to love. Love in a second sense—love as distinct from 'being in love' is not merely a feeling. It is a deep unity, maintained by the will and deliberately strengthened by habit; reinforced by (in Christian marriages) the grace which both parents ask, and receive, from God. They can have this love for each other even at those moments when they do not like each other; as you love yourself even when you do not like yourself."

3. Also from book 3, chapter 6, of *Mere Christianity*: "People get from books the idea that if you have married the right person you may expect to go on 'being in love' forever. As a result, when they find they are not, they think this proves they have made a mistake and are entitled to a change—not realizing that, when they have changed, the glamour will presently go out of the new love just as it went out of the old one. In this department, as in every other, thrills come at the beginning and do not last.... Let the thrill go—let it die away—go on through that period of death into the quieter interest and happiness that follow—and you will find you are living in a world of new thrills all the time. But if you decide to make thrills your regular diet and try to prolong them artificially, they will all get weaker and

which they call "being in love" is the only respectable ground for marriage;[2] that marriage can, and ought to, render this excitement permanent; and that a marriage which does not do so is no longer binding.[3] This idea is our parody of an idea that came from the Enemy.

The whole philosophy of Hell rests on recognition of the axiom that one thing is not another thing, and, specially, that one self is not another self. My good is my good and your good is yours. What one gains another loses. Even an inanimate object is what it is by excluding all other objects from the space it occupies; if it expands, it does so by thrusting other objects aside or by absorbing them. A self does the same. With beasts the absorption takes the form of eating; for us, it means the sucking of will and freedom out of a weaker self into a stronger. "To be" *means* "to be in competition."

Now the Enemy's philosophy is nothing more nor less than one continued attempt to evade this very obvious truth. He aims at a contradiction. Things are to be many, yet somehow also one. The good of one self is to be the good of another. This impossibility He calls *love,* and this same monotonous panacea[4] can be detected under all He does and even all He is—or claims to be. Thus He is not content, even Himself, to be a sheer arithmetical unity; He claims to be three as well as one,[5] in order that this nonsense about Love may find a foothold in His own nature. At the other end of the scale, He introduces into matter that obscene invention the organism, in which the parts are perverted from their natural destiny of competition and made to co-operate.

His real motive for fixing on sex as the method of reproduction among humans is only too apparent from the use He has made of it. Sex might have been, from our point of view, quite innocent. It might have been merely one more mode in which a stronger self preyed upon a weaker—as it is, indeed, among the spiders where the bride concludes her nuptials by eating her groom. But in the humans the Enemy has gratuitously associated affection between the parties with sexual desire. He has also made the offspring dependent on the parents and given the parents an impulse to support it—thus producing the Family, which is like the organism, only worse; for the members are more distinct, yet also united in a more

weaker, and fewer and fewer, and you will be a bored, disillusioned old man for the rest of your life."

4. Panacea: a questionable remedy for all problems.

5. In traditional Christian theology, "three as well as one" would be God the Father, God the Son (Jesus Christ), and God the Holy Spirit—the Trinity.

6. A reference to the Apostle Paul's first letter to the church in Corinth, chapter 6, verse 16: "Or do you not know that he who is joined to a prostitute becomes one body with her? For, as it is written, 'The two will become one flesh.'" Paul is quoting Genesis 2:24.

7. Transcendental: transcendent, extraordinary, mystical, beyond average experience.

conscious and responsible way. The whole thing, in fact, turns out to be simply one more device for dragging in Love.

Now comes the joke. The Enemy described a married couple as "one flesh." He did not say "a happily married couple" or "a couple who married because they were in love," but you can make the humans ignore that. You can also make them forget that the man they call Paul did not confine it to *married* couples. Mere copulation, for him, makes "one flesh."[6]

You can thus get the humans to accept as rhetorical eulogies of "being in love" what were in fact plain descriptions of the real significance of sexual intercourse. The truth is that wherever a man lies with a woman, there, whether they like it or not, a transcendental[7] relation is set up between them which must be eternally enjoyed or eternally endured. From the true statement that this transcendental relation was intended to produce, and, if obediently entered into, too often *will* produce, affection and the family, humans can be made to infer the false belief that the blend of affection, fear, and desire which they call "being in love" is the only thing that makes marriage either happy or holy. The error is easy to produce because "being in love" does very often, in Western Europe, precede marriages which are made in obedience to the Enemy's designs, that is, with the intention of fidelity, fertility, and good will; just as religious emotion very often, but not always, attends conversion. In other words, the humans are to be encouraged to regard as the basis for marriage a highly-coloured and distorted version of something the Enemy really promises as its result. Two advantages follow. In the first place, humans who have not the gift of continence[8] can be deterred from seeking marriage as a solution because they do not find themselves "in love," and, thanks to us, the idea of marrying with any other motive seems to them low and cynical. Yes, they think that. They regard the intention of loyalty to a partnership for mutual help, for the preservation of chastity, and for the transmission of life, as something lower than a storm of emotion. (Don't neglect to make your man think the marriage-service[9] very offensive.) In the second place any sexual infatuation whatever, so long as it intends marriage, will be regarded as "love," and "love" will be held to excuse a man from

8. Continence: self-restraint from yielding to impulse or desire.

9. The traditional Christian marriage service includes vows of fidelity, the commitment to one another in the best and worst of circumstances, and the hope of bearing children.

10. Wanton: a person who is immoral, unchaste, sexually indiscriminate.

all the guilt, and to protect him from all the consequences, of marrying a heathen, a fool, or a wanton.[10] But more of this in my next,

Your affectionate uncle
Screwtape

Letter 19

My dear Wormwood,

have been thinking very hard about the question in your last letter. If, as I have clearly shown, all selves are by their very nature in competition, and therefore the Enemy's idea of Love is a contradiction in terms, what becomes of my reiterated warning that He really loves the human vermin and really desires their freedom and continued existence?[1] I hope, my dear boy, you have not shown my letters to anyone. Not that it matters of course. Anyone would see that the appearance of heresy[2] into which I have fallen is purely accidental. By the way, I hope you understood, too, that some apparently uncomplimentary references to Slubgob were purely jocular. I really have the highest respect for him. And, of course, some things I said about not

First published in *The Guardian* on September 5, 1941.

1. "God, who needs nothing, loves into existence wholly superfluous creatures in order that He may love and perfect them." (*Four Loves,* chap. 6.)

2. Heresy: an opinion or doctrine that is at odds with the established beliefs of a religion.

3. Mooted: discussed, argued.

4. The crucifixion of Jesus Christ. "He [God] creates the universe, already foreseeing—or should we say 'seeing'? there are not tenses in God—the buzzing cloud of flies about the cross, the flayed back pressed against the uneven stake, the nails driven through the mesial nerves, the repeated torture of back and arms as it is time after time, for breath's sake, hitched up. . . . Herein is love." (*Four Loves,* chap. 6.)

5. Cock-and-bull: absurd or nonsensical.

6. Love that acts, asking nothing nor expecting nothing in return. In *The Four Loves,* chapter 6, Lewis calls this divine gift love: "Love Himself working in a man—is wholly disinterested and desires what is simply best for the beloved." It appears in chapter 13 of the Apostle Paul's first letter to the Corinthians as "charity" (or "love"), translated from the Greek word *agape.*

shielding you from the authorities were not seriously meant. You can trust me to look after your interests. But do keep everything under lock and key.

The truth is I slipped by mere carelessness into saying that the Enemy really loves the humans. That, of course, is an impossibility. He is one being, they are distinct from Him. Their good cannot be His. All His talk about Love must be a disguise for something else—He must have some *real* motive for creating them and taking so much trouble about them. The reason one comes to talk as if He really had this impossible Love is our utter failure to find out that real motive. What does He stand to make out of them? That is the insoluble question. I do not see that it can do any harm to tell you that this very problem was a chief cause of Our Father's quarrel with the Enemy. When the creation of man was first mooted[3] and when, even at that stage, the Enemy freely confessed that he foresaw a certain episode about a cross,[4] Our Father very naturally sought an interview and asked for an explanation. The Enemy gave no reply except to produce the cock-and-bull[5] story about disinterested love[6] which He has been circulating ever since. This Our Father naturally could not accept. He implored the Enemy to lay His cards on the table, and gave Him every opportunity. He admitted that he felt a real anxiety to know the secret; the Enemy replied "I wish with all my heart that you did." It was, I imagine, at this stage in the interview that Our Father's disgust at such an unprovoked lack of confidence caused him to remove himself an infinite distance from the Presence with a suddenness which has given rise to the ridiculous enemy story that he was forcibly thrown out of Heaven.[7] Since then, we have begun to see why our Oppressor was so secretive. His throne depends on the secret. Members of His faction have frequently admitted that if ever we came to understand what He means by Love, the war would be over and we should re-enter Heaven. And there lies the great task. We know that He cannot really love: nobody can: it doesn't make sense. If we could only find out what He is *really* up to! Hypothesis after hypothesis has been tried, and still we can't find out. Yet we must never lose hope; more and more complicated theories, fuller and fuller collections of data, richer rewards

7. Alluding to John Milton's *Paradise Lost* and Isaiah 14:12–19.

questioning
How can we enter
Heaven. When

8. Teetotalism: complete abstinence from drinking alcohol.

9. Overweening: arrogant, over-confident.

10. Asceticism: a lifestyle of self-denial and austerity designed to free the soul from the body's enslavements.

for researchers who make progress, more and more terrible punishments for those who fail—all this, pursued and accelerated to the very end of time, cannot, surely, fail to succeed.

You complain that my last letter does not make it clear whether I regard *being in love* as a desirable state for a human or not. But really, Wormwood, that is the sort of question one expects *them* to ask! Leave them to discuss whether "Love," or patriotism, or celibacy, or candles on altars, or teetotalism,[8] or education, are "good" or "bad." Can't you see there's no answer? Nothing matters at all except the tendency of a given state of mind, in given circumstances, to move a particular patient at a particular moment nearer to the Enemy or nearer to us. Thus it would be quite a good thing to make the patient decide that "love" is "good" or "bad." If he is an arrogant man with a contempt for the body really based on delicacy but mistaken by him for purity—and one who takes pleasure in flouting what most of his fellows approve—by all means let him decide against love. Instill into him an overweening[9] asceticism[10] and then, when you have separated his sexuality from all that might humanise it, weigh in on him with it in some much more brutal and cynical form. If, on the other hand, he is an emotional, gullible man, feed him on minor poets and fifth-rate novelists of the old school until you have made him believe that "Love" is both irresistible and somehow intrinsically meritorious. This belief is not much help, I grant you, in producing casual unchastity; but it is an incomparable recipe for prolonged, "noble," romantic, tragic adulteries, ending, if all goes well, in murders and suicides. Failing that, it can be used to steer the patient into a useful marriage. For marriage, though the Enemy's invention, has its uses. There must be several young women in your patient's neighbourhood who would render the Christian life intensely difficult to him if only you could persuade him to marry one of them. Please send me a report on this when you next write. In the meantime, get it quite clear in your own mind that this state of *falling in love* is not, in itself, necessarily favourable either to us or to the other side. It is simply an occasion which we and the Enemy are both trying to exploit. Like most of the other things which humans

are excited about, such as health and sickness, age and youth, or war and peace, it is,
from the point of view of the spiritual life,
mainly raw material,

Your affectionate uncle
Screwtape

Letter 20

My dear Wormwood,

First published in *The Guardian* on September 12, 1941.

I note with great displeasure that the Enemy has, for the time being, put a forcible end to your direct attacks on the patient's chastity. You ought to have known that He always does in the end, and you ought to have stopped before you reached that stage. For as things are, your man has now discovered the dangerous truth that these attacks don't last forever; consequently you cannot use again what is, after all, our best weapon—the belief of ignorant humans, that there is no hope of getting rid of us except by yielding. I suppose you've tried persuading him that chastity is unhealthy?

I haven't yet got a report from you on young women in the neighbourhood. I should like it at once, for if we can't use his sexuality to make him unchaste we must try to use it for the promotion of a desirable marriage. In the meantime I would like to give you some hint about the type of woman—I mean the physical type—which he should be encouraged to fall in love with if "falling in love" is the best we can manage.

In a rough and ready way, of course, this question is decided for us by spirits far deeper down in the Lowerarchy than you and I. It is the business of these great masters to produce in every age a general misdirection of what may be called sexual "taste." This they do by working through the small circle of popular artists, dressmakers, actresses, and advertisers who determine the fashionable type. The aim is to guide each sex away from those members of the other with whom spiritually helpful, happy, and fertile marriages are most likely. Thus we have now for many centuries triumphed over nature to the extent of making certain secondary characteristics of the male (such as the beard) disagreeable to nearly all the females—and there is more in that than you might suppose. As regards the male taste we have varied a good deal. At one time we have directed it to the statuesque and aristocratic type of beauty, mixing men's vanity with their desires and encouraging the race to breed chiefly from the most arrogant and prodigal women. At another, we have selected an exaggeratedly feminine type, faint and languishing, so that folly and cowardice, and all the general falseness and littleness of mind which go with them, shall be at a premium. At present we are on the opposite tack. The age of jazz[1] has succeeded the age of the waltz,[2] and we now teach men to like women whose bodies are scarcely distinguishable from those of boys. Since this is a kind of beauty even more transitory than most, we thus aggravate the female's chronic horror of growing old (with many excellent results) and render her less willing and less able to bear children. And that is not all. We have engineered a great increase in the licence which society allows to the representation of the apparent nude (not the real nude) in art, and its exhibition on the stage or the bathing beach. It is all a fake, of course; the figures in the popular art are falsely drawn; the real women in bathing suits or tights are actually pinched in and propped up to make them appear

1. Named by author F. Scott Fitzgerald (1896–1940), the Jazz Age—or the Roaring Twenties, as it was known in the United States—was a post–World War I period that emphasized jazz music, dance, and counterculture rebellion for women (boyish haircuts, loose tops and short skirts, cigarette smoking, flamboyant behavior). It was marked for its hedonistic and cynical tone.

2. Though the waltz as a dance can be traced back to the eighteenth century, it reached its peak of popularity in the late nineteenth century throughout Europe and the United States as it became a feature of royal and formal occasions. Arguably, the "waltz age" ended with the international upheaval of World War I.

firmer and more slender and more boyish than nature allows a full-grown woman to be. Yet at the same time, the modern world is taught to believe that it is being "frank" and "healthy" and getting back to nature. As a result we are more and more directing the desires of men to something which does not exist—making the rôle of the eye in sexuality more and more important and at the same time making its demands more and more impossible. What follows you can easily forecast!

That is the general strategy of the moment. But inside that framework you will still find it possible to encourage your patient's desires in one of two directions. You will find, if you look carefully into any human's heart, that he is haunted by at least two imaginary women—a terrestrial[3] and an infernal[4] Venus,[5] and that his desire differs qualitatively according to its object. There is one type for which his desire is such as to be naturally amenable to the Enemy—readily mixed with charity, readily obedient to marriage, coloured all through with that golden light of reverence and naturalness which we detest; there is another type which he desires brutally, and desires to desire brutally, a type best used to draw him away from marriage altogether but which, even within marriage, he would tend to treat as a slave, an idol, or an accomplice. His love for the first might involve what the Enemy calls evil, but only accidentally; the man would wish that she was not someone else's wife and be sorry that he could not love her lawfully. But in the second type, the felt evil is what he wants; it is that "tang" in the flavour which he is after. In the face, it is the visible animality, or sulkiness, or craft, or cruelty which he likes, and in the body, something quite different from what he ordinarily calls Beauty, something he may even, in a sane hour, describe as ugliness, but which, by our art, can be made to play on the raw nerve of his private obsession.

The real use of the infernal Venus is, no doubt, as prostitute or mistress. But if your man is a Christian, and if he has been well trained in nonsense about irresistible and all-excusing "Love," he can often be induced to marry her. And that is very well worth bringing about. You will have failed as regards fornication and solitary vice; but there are other, and more indirect, methods of using a man's sexuality to his undoing. And, by the way, they are not only efficient, but delightful; the unhappiness produced is of a very lasting and exquisite kind,

Your affectionate uncle
Screwtape

Letter 21

My dear Wormwood,

Yes. A period of sexual temptation is an excellent time for working in a subordinate attack on the patient's peevishness.[1] It may even be the main attack, as long as he thinks it the subordinate one. But here, as in everything else, the way must be prepared for your moral assault by darkening his intellect.

Men are not angered by mere misfortune but by misfortune conceived as injury. And the sense of injury depends on the feeling that a legitimate claim has been denied. The more claims on life, therefore, that your patient can be induced to make, the more often he will feel injured and, as a result, ill-tempered. Now you will have noticed that nothing throws him into a passion so easily as to find a tract of time which he reckoned

First published in *The Guardian* on September 19, 1941.

1. Peevishness: irritability, crankiness, pettiness.

2. Tête-à-tête: a private conversation between two people.

on having at his own disposal unexpectedly taken from him. It is the unexpected visitor (when he looked forward to a quiet evening), or the friend's talkative wife (turning up when he looked forward to a *tête-à-tête*[2] with the friend), that throw him out of gear. Now he is not yet so uncharitable or slothful that these small demands on his courtesy are *in themselves* too much for it. They anger him because he regards his time as his own and feels that it is being stolen. You must therefore zealously guard in his mind the curious assumption "My time is my own." Let him have the feeling that he starts each day as the lawful possessor of twenty-four hours. Let him feel as a grievous tax that portion of this property which he has to make over to his employers, and as a generous donation that further portion which he allows to religious duties. But what he must never be permitted to doubt is that the total from which these deductions have been made was, in some mysterious sense, his own personal birthright.

You have here a delicate task. The assumption which you want him to go on making is so absurd that, if once it is questioned, even we cannot find a shred of argument in its defence. The man can neither make, nor retain, one moment of time; it all comes to him by pure gift; he might as well regard the sun and moon as his chattels.[3] He is also, in theory, committed to a total service of the Enemy; and if the Enemy appeared to him in bodily form and demanded that total service for even one day, he would not refuse. He would be greatly relieved if that one day involved nothing harder than listening to the conversation of a foolish woman; and he would be relieved almost to the pitch of disappointment if for one half-hour in that day the Enemy said "Now you may go and amuse yourself." Now if he thinks about his assumption for a moment, even he is bound to realize that he is actually in this situation every day. When I speak of preserving this assumption in his mind, therefore, the last thing I mean you to do is to furnish him with arguments in its defence. There aren't any. Your task is purely negative. Don't let his thoughts come anywhere near it. Wrap a darkness about it, and in the centre of that darkness let his sense of ownership-in-Time lie silent, uninspected, and operative.

The sense of ownership in general is always to be encouraged. The humans are always

3. Chattel: property.

putting up claims to ownership which sound equally funny in Heaven and in Hell and we must keep them doing so. Much of the modern resistance to chastity comes from men's belief that they "own" their bodies—those vast and perilous estates, pulsating with the energy that made the worlds, in which they find themselves without their consent and from which they are ejected at the pleasure of Another! It is as if a royal child whom his father has placed, for love's sake, in titular command of some great province, under the real rule of wise counsellors, should come to fancy he really owns the cities, the forests, and the corn, in the same way as he owns the bricks on the nursery floor.

We produce this sense of ownership not only by pride but by confusion. We teach them not to notice the different senses of the possessive pronoun—the finely graded differences that run from "my boots" through "my dog," "my servant," "my wife," "my father," "my master," and "my country," to "my God." They can be taught to reduce all these senses to that of "my boots," the "my" of ownership. Even in the nursery a child can be taught to mean by "my Teddy-bear" *not* the old imagined recipient of affection to whom it stands in a special relation (for that is what the Enemy will teach them to mean if we are not careful) but "the bear I can pull to pieces if I like." And at the other end of the scale, we have taught men to say "My God" in a sense not really very different from "My boots," meaning "The God on whom I have a claim for my distinguished services and whom I exploit from the pulpit—the God I have done a corner in."[4]

And all the time the joke is that the word "Mine" in its fully possessive sense cannot be uttered by a human being about anything. In the long run either Our Father or the Enemy will say "Mine" of each thing that exists, and specially of each man. They will find out in the end, never fear, to whom their time, their souls, and their bodies really belong—certainly not to *them,* whatever happens. At present the Enemy says "Mine" of everything on the pedantic, legalistic ground that He made it: Our Father hopes in the end to say "Mine" of all things on the more realistic and dynamic ground of conquest,

Your affectionate uncle
Screwtape

4. The phrase "done a corner in" may be a variation of the nineteenth-century English phrase "to make a corner," which means "to combine in order to control the price of a given article, and thus secure enormous profits." In the modern vernacular: to corner the market, to control, to be master of (E. Cobham Brewer, *Dictionary of Phrase and Fable* [London: Cassell, 1864]).

Letter 22

My dear Wormwood,

First published in *The Guardian* on September 26, 1941.

So! Your man is in love—and in the worst kind he could possibly have fallen into—and with a girl who does not even appear in the report you sent me. You may be interested to learn that the little misunderstanding with the Secret Police which you tried to raise about some unguarded expressions in one of my letters has been tidied over. If you were reckoning on that to secure my good offices, you will find yourself mistaken. You shall pay for that as well as for your other blunders. Meanwhile I enclose a little booklet, just issued, on the new House of Correction for Incompetent Tempters. It is profusely illustrated and you will not find a dull page in it.

I have looked up this girl's dossier and am horrified at what I find. Not only a Christian but such a Christian—a vile, sneaking, simpering, demure, monosyllabic, mouse-like, watery, insignificant, virginal, bread-and-butter miss. The little brute. She makes me vomit. She stinks and scalds through the very pages of the dossier. It drives me mad, the way the world has worsened. We'd have had her to the arena in the old days. That's what her sort is made for. Not that she'd do much good there, either. A two-faced little cheat (I know the sort) who looks as if she'd faint at the sight of blood and then dies with a smile. A cheat every way. Looks as if butter wouldn't melt in her mouth[1] and yet has a satirical wit. The sort of creature who'd find *ME* funny! Filthy insipid little prude[2]—and yet ready to fall into this booby's arms like any other breeding animal. Why doesn't the Enemy blast her for it, if He's so moonstruck by virginity—instead of looking on there, grinning?

He's a hedonist[3] at heart. All those fasts and vigils and stakes and crosses are only a façade. Or only like foam on the sea shore. Out at sea, out in His sea, there is pleasure, and more pleasure. He makes no secret of it; at His right hand are "pleasures for evermore."[4] Ugh! I don't think He has the least

---

1. As if butter wouldn't melt in her mouth: falsely amiable.

2. Prude: a person excessively proper, unduly modest, easily shocked, or self-righteous about sex.

3. Hedonist: a person who subscribes to the idea that pleasure is the only intrinsic good.

4. Taken from Psalm 16:11 (King James Version): "Thou wilt show me the path of life: in thy presence is fullness of joy: at thy right hand there are pleasures for evermore."

inkling of that high and austere mystery to which we rise in the Miserific Vision.[5] He's vulgar, Wormwood. He has a bourgeois[6] mind. He has filled His world full of pleasures. There are things for humans to do all day long without His minding in the least— sleeping, washing, eating, drinking, making love, playing, praying, working. Everything has to be *twisted* before it's any use to us. We fight under cruel disadvantages.

Nothing is naturally on our side. (Not that that excuses you. I'll settle with you presently. You have always hated me and been insolent when you dared.)

Then, of course, he gets to know this woman's family and whole circle. Could you not see that the very house she lives in is one that he ought never to have entered? The whole place reeks of that deadly odour. The very gardener, though he has only been there five years, is beginning to acquire it. Even guests, after a week-end visit, carry some of the smell away with them. The dog and the cat are tainted with it. And a house full of the impenetrable mystery.[7] We are certain (it is a matter of first principles) that each member of the family must in some way be making capital out of the others—

5. As is true with everything in the world of Screwtape, if a "beatific vision" is the ultimate connection between a human and God, then a "miserific vision" is its opposite.

6. Bourgeois: boringly conventional, middle-class.

7. Impenetrable mystery: the love of God. See note 6 in "Letter 19" (p. 112).

8. Quoting George MacDonald (1824–1905) from "The Hands of the Father" in *Unspoken Sermons,* vol. 1 (London: Alexander Strahan, 1867): "And there shall be moments when, filled with that spirit which is the Lord, nothing will ease our hearts of their love but the commending of all men, all our brothers, all our sisters, to the one Father. Nor shall we ever know that repose in the Father's hands, that rest of the Holy Sepulchre, which the Lord knew when the agony of death was over, when the storm of the world died away behind his retiring spirit, and he entered the regions where there is only life, and therefore all that is not music is silence (for all noise comes of the conflict of Life and Death)—we shall never be able, I say, to rest in the bosom of the Father, till the fatherhood is fully revealed to us in the love of the brothers." Lewis also included part of this quote in *George MacDonald: An Anthology* (London: Geoffrey Bles, 1946).

but we can't find out how. They guard as jealously as the Enemy Himself the secret of what really lies behind this pretence of disinterested love. The whole house and garden is one vast obscenity. It bears a sickening resemblance to the description one human writer made of Heaven; "the regions where there is only life and therefore all that is not music is silence."[8]

Music and silence—how I detest them both! How thankful we should be that ever since our Father entered Hell—though longer ago than humans, reckoning in light years, could express—no square inch of infernal space and no moment of infernal time has been surrendered to either of those abominable forces, but all has been occupied by Noise—Noise, the grand dynamism, the audible expression of all that is exultant, ruthless, and virile—Noise which alone defends us from silly qualms, despairing scruples, and impossible desires. We will make the whole universe a noise in the end. We have already made great strides in this direction as regards the Earth. The melodies and silences of Heaven will be shouted down in the end. But I admit we are not yet loud enough, or anything like it. Research is in progress. Meanwhile *you,* disgusting little—

[Here the MS breaks off and is resumed in a different hand.]

In the heat of composition I find that I have inadvertently allowed myself to assume the form of a large centipede.[9] I am accordingly dictating the rest to my secretary. Now that the transformation is complete I recognise it as a periodical phenomenon. Some rumour of it has reached the humans and a distorted account of it appears in the poet Milton,[10] with the ridiculous addition that such changes of shape are a "punishment" imposed on us by the Enemy. A more modern writer—someone with a name like Pshaw[11]—has, however, grasped the truth. Transformation proceeds from within and is a glorious manifestation of that Life Force[12] which Our Father would worship if he worshipped anything but himself. In my present form I feel even more anxious to see you, to unite you to myself in an indissoluble embrace,

(Signed) TOADPIPE
For his Abysmal Sublimity Under Secretary Screwtape, TE, BS, etc.

9. It may be a remarkable coincidence that G. K. Chesterton (1874–1936), who had a significant influence on C. S. Lewis, also wrote extensively about George Bernard Shaw (see note 1 in "Letter 7", p. 40) with whom he had an adversarial friendship. In one case, he wryly defended the "plain, pugnacious style of Shaw" as monosyllabic, which has "slain the polysyllable, that huge and slimy centipede which has sprawled over all the valleys of England like the 'loathly worm' who was slain by the ancient knight. He does not think that difficult questions will be made simpler by using difficult words about them." (G. K. Chesterton, *George Bernard Shaw* [New York: John Lane, 1909], p. 239.)

10. John Milton (1608–1674), English poet. In his *Paradise Lost,* book 10, the demons raged against God—and were turned into snakes.

11. A satirical reference to Anglo-Irish playwright and philosopher George Bernard Shaw (1856–1950), best known for *Man and Superman, Pygmalion, Androcles and the Lion,* and *Major Barbara* (to name only a few). For more on this reference and the "Life Force," see note 1 in "Letter 7" (p. 40).

12. See note 1 in "Letter 7" (p. 40).

Letter 23

My dear Wormwood,

Through this girl and her disgusting family the patient is now getting to know more Christians every day, and very intelligent Christians too. For a long time it will be quite impossible to *remove* spirituality from his life. Very well then; we must *corrupt* it. No doubt you have often practised transforming yourself into an angel of light as a parade-ground exercise. Now is the time to do it in the face of the Enemy. The World and the Flesh[1] have failed us; a third Power[2] remains. And success of this third kind is the most glorious of all. A spoiled saint, a Pharisee, an inquisitor, or a magician, makes better sport in Hell than a mere common tyrant or debauchee.

Looking round your patient's new friends I find that the best point of attack would

First published in *The Guardian* on October 3, 1941, with the title "The Historical Jesus."

1. References a collect (a short prayer, often specific to a day, season, or church occasion) from the Book of Common Prayer: "Lord, we beseech thee, grant thy people grace to withstand the temptations of the world, the flesh, and the devil, and with pure hearts and minds to follow thee the only God."

2. Presumably the "third power" is religion itself. Lewis elucidates on this idea further in *Screwtape Proposes a Toast* and concludes with: "All said and done, my friends, it will be an ill day for us if what most humans mean by 'religion' ever vanishes from the Earth. It can still send us the truly delicious sins. The fine flower of unholiness can grow only in the close neighbourhood of the Holy. Nowhere do we tempt so successfully as on the very steps of the altar."

be the border-line between theology and politics. Several of his new friends are very much alive to the social implications of their religion. That, in itself, is a bad thing; but good can be made out of it.

You will find that a good many Christian-political writers think that Christianity began going wrong, and departing from the doctrine of its Founder, at a very early stage. Now this idea must be used by us to encourage once again the conception of a "historical Jesus" to be found by clearing away later "accretions[3] and perversions" and then to be contrasted with the whole Christian tradition. In the last generation we promoted the construction of such a "historical Jesus" on liberal and humanitarian lines; we are now putting forward a new "historical Jesus" on Marxian, catastrophic, and revolutionary lines. The advantages of these constructions, which we intend to change every thirty years or so, are manifold. In the first place they all tend to direct men's devotion to something which does not exist, for each "historical Jesus" is unhistorical. The documents say what they say and cannot be added to; each new "historical Jesus" therefore has to be got out of them by suppression at one point and exaggeration at another, and by that sort of guessing (*brilliant* is the adjective we teach humans to apply to it) on which no one would risk ten shillings[4] in ordinary life, but which is enough to produce a crop of new Napoleons,[5] new Shakespeares,[6] and new Swifts,[7] in every publisher's autumn list.[8] In the second place, all such constructions place the importance of their historical Jesus in some peculiar theory He is supposed to have promulgated.[9] He has to be a "great man" in the modern sense of the word—one standing at the terminus of some centrifugal and unbalanced line of thought—a crank vending a panacea. We thus distract men's minds from who He is, and what He did. We first make Him solely a teacher,[10] and then conceal the very substantial agreement between His teachings and those of all other great moral teachers. For humans must not be allowed to notice that all great moralists are sent by the Enemy not to inform men but to remind them, to restate the primeval moral platitudes against our continual concealment of them. We make the Sophists:[11] He raises up a Socrates[12] to answer them. Our third

4. Shilling: a form of British currency, valued at twelve pence to the shilling and twenty shillings to the pound, but discontinued in 1971 due to the decimalization of British money. In this context, it suggests that a person wouldn't normally risk anything of value.

5. Napoleon Bonaparte (1769–1821) was a French military leader who assumed political power toward the end of the French Revolution.

6. English poet and playwright William Shakespeare (1564–1616).

7. Jonathan Swift (1667–1745) was an Irish novelist, satirist, political activist, and essayist. He is best known for his satirical novel *Gulliver's Travels*.

8. Publisher's list: announcement by publishers of forthcoming published titles.

9. Promulgate: to declare publicly, promote.

10. Lewis famously dismantled this view in "What Are We to Make of Jesus?": "The idea of a great moral teacher saying what Christ said is out of the question. In my opinion, the only person who can say that sort of thing is either God or a complete lunatic suffering from that form of delusion which undermines the whole mind of man. . . . We may note in passing that He was never regarded as a mere moral teacher. He did not produce that effect on any of the people who actually met Him. He produced mainly three effects— Hatred—Terror—Adoration. There was no trace of people expressing mild approval." (*God in the Dock.*) And from book 2, chapter 3, of *Mere Christianity*: "You can shut Him up for a fool, you can spit at Him and kill Him as a demon; or you can fall at his feet and call Him Lord and God. But let us not come with any patronizing nonsense about His being a great human teacher. He has not left that open to us. He did not intend to."

11. Sophists were paid itinerant teachers in ancient Greece who used rhetoric and a mastery of language to instruct and lecture, even boasting that they could answer any question put to them. Socrates and Plato both debated with the sophists. They were particularly popular among young men aspiring to political office. Centuries later, "sophist" was equated with a person who used exceptionally clever talk to deceive others. The words "sopho" and "sophia" are Greek for "wisdom."

12. Socrates (469–399 BC) was a classical Greek philosopher who has been acknowledged as one of the founders of Western philosophy. Lewis was a founding member and president of the Oxford Socratic Club from 1942 to 1954.

13. This "universal moral law" was also known as "natural law," which refers to the belief that humanity is aware of, and subject to, an objective and common understanding of morality, ethics, rights, and values. Lewis explores this topic, using various names for it, in the first five chapters of *Mere Christianity,* in *The Abolition of Man,* and throughout his fiction (particularly his Space Trilogy).

aim is, by these constructions, to destroy the devotional life. For the real presence of the Enemy, otherwise experienced by men in prayer and sacrament, we substitute a merely probable, remote, shadowy, and uncouth figure, one who spoke a strange language and died a long time ago. Such an object cannot in fact be worshipped. Instead of the Creator adored by its creature, you soon have merely a leader acclaimed by a partisan, and finally a distinguished character approved by a judicious historian. And fourthly, besides being unhistorical in the Jesus it depicts, religion of this kind is false to history in another sense. No nation, and few individuals, are really brought into the Enemy's camp by the historical study of the biography of Jesus, simply as biography. Indeed materials for a full biography have been withheld from men. The earliest converts were converted by a single historical fact (the Resurrection) and a single theological doctrine (the Redemption) operating on a sense of sin which they already had—and sin, not against some new fancy-dress law produced as a novelty by a "great man," but against the old, platitudinous, universal moral law[13] which they had been taught by their nurses and mothers. The "Gospels" come later and were written not to make Christians but to edify Christians already made.

The "historical Jesus" then, however dangerous he may seem to be to us at some particular point, is always to be encouraged. About the general connection between Christianity and politics, our position is more delicate. Certainly we do not want men to allow their Christianity to flow over into their political life, for the establishment of anything like a really just society would be a major disaster. On the other hand we do want, and want very much, to make men treat Christianity as a means; preferably, of course, as a means to their own advancement, but, failing that, as a means to anything—even to social justice. The thing to do is to get a man at first to value social justice as a thing which the Enemy demands, and then work him on to the stage at which he values Christianity because it may produce social justice. For the Enemy will not be used as a convenience. Men or nations who think they can revive the Faith in order to make a good society might just as well think they can use the stairs of Heaven

14. Chemist's shop: a drugstore or pharmacy.

15. A quote from American theologian Reinhold Niebuhr (1892–1971), *An Interpretation of Christian Ethics* (New York and London: Harper and Brothers, 1935).

as a short cut to the nearest chemist's shop.[14] Fortunately it is quite easy to coax humans round this little corner. Only today I have found a passage in a Christian writer where he recommends his own version of Christianity on the ground that "only such a faith can outlast the death of old cultures and the birth of new civilisations."[15] You see the little rift? "Believe this, not because it is true, but for some other reason." That's the game,

Your affectionate uncle
Screwtape

Letter 24

My dear Wormwood,

have been in correspondence with Slumtrimpet who is in charge of your patient's young woman, and begin to see the chink in her armour. It is an unobtrusive little vice which she shares with nearly all women who have grown up in an intelligent circle united by a clearly defined belief; and it consists in a quite untroubled assumption that the outsiders who do not share this belief are really too stupid and ridiculous.[1] The males, who habitually meet these outsiders, do not feel that way; their confidence, if they are confident, is of a different kind. Hers, which she supposes to be due to Faith, is in reality largely due to the mere colour she has taken from her surroundings. It is not, in fact, very different from the conviction she would have felt at

First published in *The Guardian* on October 10, 1941, with the title "Spiritual Pride."

1. Lewis deals with the subject of exclusive groups and cliques in his essay "The Inner Ring," found in *The Weight of Glory and Other Addresses.*

2. Fish-knives: cutlery for de-boning and eating fish.

3. Venial: able to be forgiven, pardonable, a minor sin.

the age of ten that the kind of fish-knives[2] used in her father's house were the proper or normal or "real" kind, while those of the neighbouring families were "not real fish-knives" at all. Now the element of ignorance and naïvety in all this is so large, and the element of spiritual pride so small, that it gives us little hope of the girl herself. But have you thought of how it can be made to influence your own patient?

It is always the novice who exaggerates. The man who has risen in society is over-refined, the young scholar is pedantic. In this new circle your patient is a novice. He is there daily meeting Christian life of a quality he never before imagined and seeing it all through an enchanted glass because he is in love. He is anxious (indeed the Enemy commands him) to imitate this quality. Can you get him to imitate this *defect* in his mistress and to exaggerate it until what was venial[3] in her becomes in him the strongest and most beautiful of the vices—Spiritual Pride?

The conditions seem ideally favourable. The new circle in which he finds himself is one of which he is tempted to be proud for many reasons other than its Christianity. It is a better educated, more intelligent, more agreeable society than any he has yet encountered. He is also under some degree of illusion as to his own place in it. Under the influence of "love" he may still think himself unworthy of the girl, but he is rapidly ceasing to think himself unworthy of the others. He has no notion how much in him is forgiven because they are charitable and made the best of because he is now one of the family. He does not dream how much of his conversation, how many of his opinions, are recognised by them all as mere echoes of their own. Still less does he suspect how much of the delight he takes in these people is due to the erotic enchantment which the girl, for him, spreads over all her surroundings. He thinks that he likes their talk and way of life because of some congruity between their spiritual state and his, when in fact they are so far beyond him that if he were not in love he would be merely puzzled and repelled by much which he now accepts. He is like a dog which should imagine it understood fire-arms because its hunting instinct and love for its master enable it to enjoy a day's shooting!

Here is your chance. While the Enemy, by means of sexual love and of some very agreeable people far advanced in His service, is drawing the young barbarian up to levels he could never otherwise have reached, you must make him feel that he is finding his *own* level—that these people are "his sort" and that, coming among them, he has come home. When he turns from them to other society he will find it dull; partly because almost any society within his reach is, in fact, much less entertaining, but still more because he will miss the enchantment of the young woman. You must teach him to mistake this contrast between the circle that delights and the circle that bores him for the contrast between Christians and unbelievers. He must be made to feel (he'd better not put it into words) "how different we Christians are"; and by "we Christians" he must really, but unknowingly, mean "my set"; and by "my set" he must mean not "The people who, in their charity and humility, have accepted me," but "The people with whom I associate by right."

Success here depends on confusing him. If you try to make him explicitly and professedly proud of being a Christian, you will probably fail; the Enemy's warnings are too well known. If, on the other hand, you let the idea of "we Christians" drop out altogether and merely make him complacent about "his set," you will produce not true spiritual pride but mere social vanity which, by comparison, is a trumpery, puny little sin. What you want is to keep a sly self-congratulation mixing with all his thoughts and never allow him to raise the question "What, precisely, am I congratulating myself *about*?" The idea of belonging to an inner ring, of being in a secret, is very sweet to him. Play on that nerve. Teach him, using the influence of this girl when she is silliest, to adopt an air of *amusement* at the things the unbelievers say. Some theories which he may meet in modern Christian circles may here prove helpful; theories, I mean, that place the hope of society in some inner ring of "clerks," some trained minority of theocrats.[4] It is no affair of yours whether those theories are true or false; the great thing is to make Christianity a mystery religion in which he feels himself one of the initiates.

Pray do not fill your letters with rubbish about this European War. Its final issue is,

4. Theocrat: member of a government run by God.

no doubt, important, but that is a matter for the High Command. I am not in the least interested in knowing how many people in England have been killed by bombs. In what state of mind they died, I can learn from the office at this end. That they were going to die sometime, I knew already. Please keep your mind on your work,

Your affectionate uncle
Screwtape

Letter 25

My dear Wormwood,

The real trouble about the set your patient is living in is that it is *merely* Christian. They all have individual interests, of course, but the bond remains mere Christianity.[1] What we want, if men become Christians at all, is to keep them in the state of mind I call "Christianity And." You know—Christianity and the Crisis, Christianity and the New Psychology, Christianity and the New Order, Christianity and Faith Healing, Christianity and Psychical Research, Christianity and Vegetarianism, Christianity and Spelling Reform. If they must be Christians let them at least be Christians with a difference. Substitute for the faith itself some Fashion with a Christian coloring. Work on their horror of the Same Old Thing.

First published in *The Guardian* on October 17, 1941, with the title "The Enemy Loves Platitudes."

1. The phrase "mere Christianity" was originally used by English Puritan and theologian Richard Baxter (1615–1691) in his book *The Saints' Everlasting Rest* (1650). By Lewis's definition, it is what Christians have commonly believed at all times. He explains the concept further in the preface to *Mere Christianity*.

2. Days declared by the traditional church for fasting—abstaining from food, drink, or both.

3. Days declared by the traditional church for religious celebration.

The horror of the Same Old Thing is one of the most valuable passions we have produced in the human heart—an endless source of heresies in religion, folly in counsel, infidelity in marriage, and inconstancy in friendship. The humans live in time, and experience reality successively. To experience much of it, therefore, they must experience many different things; in other words, they must experience change. And since they need change, the Enemy (being a hedonist at heart) has made change pleasurable to them, just as He has made eating pleasurable. But since He does not wish them to make change, any more than eating, an end in itself, He has balanced the love of change in them by a love of permanence. He has contrived to gratify both tastes together in the very world He has made, by that union of change and permanence which we call Rhythm. He gives them the seasons, each season different yet every year the same, so that spring is always felt as a novelty yet always as the recurrence of an immemorial theme. He gives them in His Church a spiritual year; they change from a fast[2] to a feast,[3] but it is the same feast as before.

Now just as we pick out and exaggerate the pleasure of eating to produce gluttony, so we pick out this natural pleasantness of change and twist it into a demand for absolute novelty. This demand is entirely our workmanship. If we neglect our duty, men will be not only contented but transported by the mixed novelty and familiarity of snowdrops *this* January, sunrise *this* morning, plum pudding *this* Christmas. Children, until we have taught them better, will be perfectly happy with a seasonal round of games in which conkers[4] succeed hopscotch[5] as regularly as autumn follows summer. Only by our incessant efforts is the demand for infinite, or unrhythmical, change kept up.

This demand is valuable in various ways. In the first place it diminishes pleasure while increasing desire. The pleasure of novelty is by its very nature more subject than any other to the law of diminishing returns. And continued novelty costs money, so that the desire for it spells avarice or unhappiness or both. And again, the more rapacious this desire, the sooner it must eat up all the innocent sources of pleasure and pass on to those the Enemy forbids. Thus by inflaming

4. Conkers is a traditional English children's game played with the seeds of horse-chestnut trees.

5. Hopscotch is a popular playground game for children involving hopping over squares.

6. Gunwale: the top edge of the side of a boat, so named because guns, or weapons, were often attached there. Pronounced "gunnal."

7. Byronic: self-indulgent behavior in the manner of Lord Byron, the Romantic poet. See note 5 in "Letter 13" (p. 76).

the horror of the Same Old Thing we have recently made the Arts, for example, less dangerous to us than perhaps, they have ever been, "low-brow" and "high-brow" artists alike being now daily drawn into fresh, and still fresh, excesses of lasciviousness, unreason, cruelty, and pride. Finally, the desire for novelty is indispensable if we are to produce Fashions or Vogues.

The use of Fashions in thought is to distract the attention of men from their real dangers. We direct the fashionable outcry of each generation against those vices of which it is least in danger and fix its approval on the virtue nearest to that vice which we are trying to make endemic. The game is to have them all running about with fire extinguishers whenever there is a flood, and all crowding to that side of the boat which is already nearly gunwale[6] under. Thus we make it fashionable to expose the dangers of enthusiasm at the very moment when they are all really becoming worldly and lukewarm; a century later, when we are really making them all Byronic[7] and drunk with emotion, the fashionable outcry is directed against the dangers of the mere "understanding." Cruel ages are put on their guard against Sentimentality, feckless and idle ones against Respectability, lecherous ones against Puritanism; and whenever all men are really hastening to be slaves or tyrants we make Liberalism[8] the prime bogey.[9]

But the greatest triumph of all is to elevate this horror of the Same Old Thing into a philosophy so that nonsense in the intellect may reinforce corruption in the will. It is here that the general Evolutionary or Historical character of modern European thought (partly our work) comes in so useful. The Enemy loves platitudes. Of a proposed course of action He wants men, so far as I can see, to ask very simple questions; is it righteous? is it prudent? is it possible? Now if we can keep men asking "Is it in accordance with the general movement of our time? Is it progressive or reactionary? Is this the way that History is going?" they will neglect the relevant questions. And the questions they *do* ask are, of course, unanswerable; for they do not know the future, and what the future will be depends very largely on just those choices which they now invoke the future to help them to make. As a result, while their minds are buzzing in this vacuum, we have the better chance to

8. Liberalism, in this case, is referring to the belief in liberty and equal rights.

9. Bogey: an evil spirit, a cause of trouble, an enemy.

slip in and bend them to the action *we* have decided on. And great work has already been done. Once they knew that some changes were for the better, and others for the worse, and others again indifferent. We have largely removed this knowledge. For the descriptive adjective "unchanged" we have substituted the emotional adjective "stagnant." We have trained them to think of the Future as a promised land which favoured heroes attain—not as something which everyone reaches at the rate of sixty minutes an hour, whatever he does, whoever he is,

Your affectionate uncle
Screwtape

Letter 26

My dear Wormwood,

Yes; courtship is the time for sowing those seeds which will grow up ten years later into domestic hatred. The enchantment of unsatisfied desire produces results which the humans can be made to mistake for the results of charity. Avail yourself of the ambiguity in the word "Love": let them think they have solved by Love problems they have in fact only waived or postponed under the influence of the enchantment. While it lasts you have your chance to foment the problems in secret and render them chronic.

The grand problem is that of "unselfishness."[1] Note, once again, the admirable work of our Philological Arm in substituting the negative unselfishness for the Enemy's positive Charity. Thanks to this you can,

First published in *The Guardian* on October 24, 1941, with the title "The Generous Conflict Illusion."

1. "If you asked twenty good men today what they thought the highest of the virtues, nineteen of them would reply, Unselfishness. But if you asked almost any of the great Christians of old he would have replied, Love. You see what has happened? A negative term has been substituted for a positive, and this is of more than philological importance. . . . The New Testament has lots to say about self-denial, but not about self-denial as an end in itself. We are told to deny ourselves and to take up our crosses in order that we may follow Christ; and nearly every description of what we shall ultimately find if we do so contains an appeal to desire. If there lurks in most modern minds the notion that to desire our own good and earnestly to hope for the enjoyment of it is a bad thing, I submit that this notion has crept in from Kant [1724–1804, German philosopher] and the Stoics [Greek philosophy based on freedom from passionate emotions] and is no part of the Christian faith. Indeed, if we consider the unblushing promises of reward and the staggering nature of the rewards promised in the Gospels, it would seem that Our Lord finds our desires, not too strong, but too weak. We are half-hearted creatures, fooling about with drink and sex and ambition when infinite joy is offered us. . . . We are far too easily pleased." (*Weight of Glory*.)

from the very outset, teach a man to surrender benefits not that others may be happy in having them but that he may be unselfish in forgoing them. That is a great point gained. Another great help, where the parties concerned are male and female, is the divergence of view about Unselfishness which we have built up between the sexes. A woman means by Unselfishness chiefly taking trouble for others; a man means not giving trouble to others. As a result, a woman who is quite far gone in the Enemy's service will make a nuisance of herself on a larger scale than any man except those whom Our Father has dominated completely; and, conversely, a man will live long in the Enemy's camp before he undertakes as much spontaneous work to please others as a quite ordinary woman may do every day. Thus while the woman thinks of doing good offices and the man of respecting other people's rights, each sex, without any obvious unreason, can and does regard the other as radically selfish.

On top of these confusions you can now introduce a few more. The erotic enchantment produces a mutual complaisance in which each is *really* pleased to give in to the wishes of the other. They also know that the Enemy demands of them a degree of charity which, if attained, would result in similar actions. You must make them establish as a Law for their whole married life that degree of mutual self-sacrifice which is at present sprouting naturally out of the enchantment, but which, when the enchantment dies away, they will not have charity enough to enable them to perform. They will not see the trap, since they are under the double blindness of mistaking sexual excitement for charity and of thinking that the excitement will last.

When once a sort of official, legal, or nominal Unselfishness has been established as a rule—a rule for the keeping of which their emotional resources have died away and their spiritual resources have not yet grown—the most delightful results follow. In discussing any joint action, it becomes obligatory that A should argue in favour of B's supposed wishes and against his own, while B does the opposite. It is often impossible to find out either party's real wishes; with luck, they end by doing something that neither wants, while each feels a glow of self-righteousness and harbours a secret claim to preferential treatment for the unselfishness shown and a secret grudge against the other for the ease with which the sacrifice has been accepted. Later on you can venture on what may be called the Generous Conflict Illusion. This game is best played with more than two players, in a family with grown-up children for example. Something quite trivial, like having tea in the garden, is proposed. One member takes care to make it quite clear (though not in so many words) that he would rather not but is, of course, prepared to do so out of "Unselfishness." The others instantly withdraw their proposal, ostensibly through their "Unselfishness," but really because they don't want to be used as a sort of lay figure on which the first speaker practices petty altruisms. But he is not going to be done out of his debauch of Unselfishness either. He insists on doing "what the others want." They insist on doing what he wants. Passions are roused. Soon someone is saying "Very well then, I won't have any tea at all!" and a real quarrel ensues with bitter resentment on both sides. You see how it is done? If each side had been frankly contending for its own real wish, they would all have kept within the bounds of reason and courtesy; but just because the contention is reversed and each side is fighting the other side's battle, all the bitterness which really flows from thwarted self-righteousness and obstinacy and the accumulated grudges of the last ten years is concealed from them by the nominal or official "Unselfishness" of what they are doing or, at least, held to be excused by it. Each side is, indeed, quite alive to the cheap quality of the adversary's Unselfishness and of the false position into which he is trying to force them; but each manages to feel blameless and ill-used itself, with no more dishonesty than comes natural to a human.

A sensible human[2] once said, "If people knew how much ill-feeling Unselfishness occasions, it would not be so often recommended from the pulpit"; and again, "She's the sort of woman who lives for others— you can always tell the others by their hunted expression." All this can be begun even in the period of courtship. A little *real* selfishness on your patient's part is often of less value in the long run, for securing his soul, than the first beginnings of that elaborate and self-conscious unselfishness which may one day blossom into the sort of thing

2. The "sensible human" is unidentified.

I have described. Some degree of mutual falseness, some surprise that the girl does not always notice just how Unselfish he is being, can be smuggled in already. Cherish these things, and, above all, don't let the young fools notice them. If they notice them they will be on the road to discovering that "love" is not enough, that charity is needed and not yet achieved and that no external law can supply its place. I wish Slumtrimpet could do something about undermining that young woman's sense of the ridiculous,

Your affectionate uncle
Screwtape

Letter 27

My dear Wormwood,

ou seem to be doing very little good at present. The use of his "love" to distract his mind from the Enemy is, of course, obvious, but you reveal what poor use you are making of it when you say that the whole question of distraction and the wandering mind has now become one of the chief subjects of his prayers. That means you have largely failed. When this, or any other distraction, crosses his mind you ought to encourage him to thrust it away by sheer will power and to try to continue the normal prayer as if nothing had happened; once he accepts the distraction as his present problem and lays *that* before the Enemy and makes it the main theme of his prayers and his endeavours, then, so far from doing good, you have done harm. Anything, even

First published in *The Guardian* on October 31, 1941, with the title "The Historical Point of View."

a sin, which has the total effect of moving him close up to the Enemy, makes against us in the long run.

A promising line is the following. Now that he is in love, a new idea of *earthly* happiness has arisen in his mind: and hence a new urgency in his purely petitionary prayers[1]—about this war and other such matters. Now is the time for raising intellectual difficulties about prayer of that sort. False spirituality is always to be encouraged. On the seemingly pious ground that "praise and communion with God is the true prayer" humans can often be lured into direct disobedience to the Enemy who (in His usual flat, commonplace, uninteresting way) has definitely told them to pray for their daily bread and the recovery of their sick. You will, of course, conceal from him the fact that the prayer for daily bread, interpreted in a "spiritual sense," is really just as crudely petitionary as it is in any other sense.

But since your patient has contracted the terrible habit of obedience, he will probably continue such "crude" prayers whatever you do. But you can worry him with the haunting suspicion that the practice is

1. Petitionary prayers: appeals and requests to God.

absurd and can have no objective result. Don't forget to use the "heads I win, tails you lose" argument. If the thing he prays for doesn't happen, then that is one more proof that petitionary prayers don't work; if it does happen, he will, of course, be able to see some of the physical causes which led up to it, and "therefore it would have happened anyway," and thus a granted prayer becomes just as good a proof as a denied one that prayers are ineffective.[2]

You, being a spirit, will find it difficult to understand how he gets into this confusion. But you must remember that he takes Time for an ultimate reality. He supposes that the Enemy, like himself, sees some things as present, remembers others as past, and anticipates others as future; or even if he believes that the Enemy does not see things that way, yet, in his heart of hearts, he regards this as a peculiarity of the Enemy's mode of perception—he doesn't really think (though he would say he did) that things as the Enemy sees them are things as they are! If you tried to explain to him that men's prayers today are one of the innumerable co-ordinates with which the Enemy harmonises the weather

2. "Prayer is request. The essence of request, as distinct from compulsion, is that it may or may not be granted. And if an infinitely wise Being listens to the requests of finite and foolish creatures, of course He will sometimes grant and sometimes refuse them." (*World's Last Night,* "The Efficacy of Prayer.")

3. "I think we must take a leaf out of the scientists' book. They are quite familiar with the fact that for example, Light has to be regarded *both* as a wave and as a stream of particles. No one can make these two views consistent. Of course reality must be self-consistent; but till (if ever) we can *see* the consistency it is better to hold two inconsistent views than to ignore one side of the evidence. The real inter-relation between God's omnipotence and Man's freedom is something we can't find out." (Letter dated August 3, 1953, in *Collected Letters III*.)

of tomorrow, he would reply that then the Enemy always knew men were going to make those prayers and, if so, they did not pray freely but were predestined to do so.[3] And he would add that the weather on a given day can be traced back through its causes to the original creation of matter itself—so that the whole thing, both on the human and on the material side, is given "from the word go." What he ought to say, of course, is obvious to us; that the problem of adapting the particular weather to the particular prayers is merely the appearance, at two points in his temporal mode of perception, of the total problem of adapting the whole spiritual universe to the whole corporeal universe; that creation in its entirety operates at every point of space and time, or rather that their kind of consciousness forces them to encounter the whole, self-consistent creative act as a series of successive events. *Why* that creative act leaves room for their free will is the problem of problems, the secret behind the Enemy's nonsense about "Love." *How* it does so is no problem at all; for the enemy does not *foresee* the humans making their free contributions in a future, but *sees* them doing so in His unbounded Now. And obviously to watch a man doing something is not to make him do it.

It may be replied that some meddlesome human writers, notably Boethius,[4] have let this secret out. But in the intellectual climate which we have at last succeeded in producing throughout Western Europe, you needn't bother about that. Only the learned read old books[5] and we have now so dealt with the learned that they are of all men the least likely to acquire wisdom by doing so. We have done this by inculcating the Historical Point of View. The Historical Point of View, put briefly, means that when a learned man is presented with any statement in an ancient author, the one question he never asks is whether it is true. He asks who influenced the ancient writer, and how far the statement is consistent with what he said in other books, and what phase in the writer's development, or in the general history of thought, it illustrates, and how it affected later writers, and how often it has been misunderstood (specially by the learned man's own colleagues) and what the general course of criticism on it has been for the last ten years, and what is the

4. Anicius Manlius Severinus Boethius (480–524) was a Roman statesman and philosopher. While a prisoner of the Ostrogothic king Theodoric the Great, he wrote *The Consolation of Philosophy* (524), which explores questions of free will and predestination. Lewis discussed Boethius further in chapter 4 of *The Discarded Image* and called *The Consolation of Philosophy* "one of the most influential books ever written in Latin."

5. In the essay "On the Reading of Old Books," Lewis warned of a "blindness" that comes from reading only modern books. "Where they are true they will give us truths which we half knew already. Where they are false they will aggravate the error with which we are already dangerously ill. The only palliative is to keep the clean sea breeze of the centuries blowing through our minds, and this can be done only by reading old books." (*God in the Dock.*)

6. Henry Ford (1863–1947), of motorcar fame, said in an interview, "History is more or less bunk. We don't want tradition. We want to live in the present and the only history that is worth a tinker's dam is the history we made today" (*Chicago Tribune,* May 25, 1916).

"present state of the question." To regard the ancient writer as a possible source of knowledge—to anticipate that what he said could possibly modify your thoughts or your behaviour—this would be rejected as unutterably simple-minded. And since we cannot deceive the whole human race all the time, it is most important thus to cut every generation off from all others; for where learning makes a free commerce between the ages there is always the danger that the characteristic errors of one may be corrected by the characteristic truths of another. But thanks be to our Father and the Historical Point of View, great scholars are now as little nourished by the past as the most ignorant mechanic who holds that "history is bunk."[6]

Your affectionate uncle
Screwtape

Letter 28

My dear Wormwood,

First published in *The Guardian* on November 7, 1941.

When I told you not to fill your letters with rubbish about the war, I meant, of course, that I did not want to have your rather infantile rhapsodies about the death of men and the destruction of cities. In so far as the war really concerns the spiritual state of the patient, I naturally want full reports. And on this aspect you seem singularly obtuse. Thus you tell me with glee that there is reason to expect heavy air raids on the town where the creature lives. This is a crying example of something I have complained about already—your readiness to forget the main point in your immediate enjoyment of human suffering. Do you not know that bombs kill men? Or do you not realize that the patient's death, at this moment, is precisely what we want to avoid? He has escaped the worldly friends with whom you tried to entangle him; he has "fallen in love" with a very Christian woman and is temporarily immune from your attacks on his chastity; and the various methods of corrupting his spiritual life which we have been trying are so far unsuccessful. At the present moment, as the full impact of the war draws nearer and his worldly hopes take a proportionately lower place in his mind, full of his defence work, full of the girl, forced to attend to his neighbours more than he has ever done before and liking it more than he expected, "taken out of himself" as the humans say, and daily increasing in conscious dependence on the Enemy, he will almost certainly be lost to us if he is killed tonight. This is so obvious that I am ashamed to write it. I sometimes wonder if you young fiends are not kept out on temptation-duty too long at a time—if you are not in some danger of becoming infected by the sentiments and values of the humans among whom you work. They, of course, do tend to regard death as the prime evil and survival as the greatest good. But that is because we have taught them to do so. Do not let us be infected by our own propaganda. I know it seems strange that your chief aim at the moment should be the very same thing for which the patient's lover and his mother are praying—namely his bodily safety. But so it is; you should be guarding him like the apple of your eye. If he dies now, you lose him. If he survives the war, there is always hope. The Enemy has guarded him from you through the first great wave of temptations. But, if only he can be kept alive, you have time itself for your ally. The long, dull monotonous years of middle-aged prosperity or middle-aged adversity are excellent campaigning weather.[1] You see, it is so hard for these creatures to *persevere*. The routine of adversity, the gradual decay of youthful loves and youthful hopes, the quiet despair (hardly felt as pain) of ever overcoming the chronic temptations with which we have again and again defeated them, the drabness which we create in their lives and the inarticulate resentment with which we teach them to respond to it—all this provides admirable opportunities of wearing out a soul by attrition. If, on the other hand, the middle years prove prosperous, our position is even stronger. Prosperity knits a man

1. Campaigning weather: a good day for battle. And it's worth noting that Lewis was in his early forties when he wrote *The Screwtape Letters*.

to the World. He feels that he is "finding his place in it," while really it is finding its place in him. His increasing reputation, his widening circle of acquaintances, his sense of importance, the growing pressure of absorbing and agreeable work, build up in him a sense of being really at home in earth which is just what we want. You will notice that the young are generally less unwilling to die than the middle-aged and the old.

The truth is that the Enemy, having oddly destined these mere animals to life in His own eternal world, has guarded them pretty effectively from the danger of feeling at home anywhere else. That is why we must often wish long life to our patients; seventy years is not a day too much for the difficult task of unravelling their souls from Heaven and building up a firm attachment to the earth. While they are young we find them always shooting off at a tangent. Even if we contrive to keep them ignorant of explicit religion, the incalculable winds of fantasy and music and poetry— the mere face of a girl, the song of a bird, or the sight of a horizon—are always blowing our whole structure away. They *will* not apply themselves steadily to worldly advancement, prudent connections, and the policy of safety first. So inveterate[2] is their appetite for Heaven that our best method, at this stage, of attaching them to earth is to make them believe that earth can be turned into Heaven at some future date by politics, or eugenics,[3] or "science," or psychology, or what not. Real worldliness is a work of time—assisted, of course, by pride, for we teach them to describe the creeping death as good sense or Maturity or Experience. *Experience,* in the peculiar sense we teach them to give it, is, by the by, a most useful word. A great human philosopher nearly let our secret out when he said that where Virtue is concerned "Experience is the mother of illusion";[4] but thanks to a change in Fashion, and also, of course, to the Historical Point of View, we have largely rendered his book innocuous.

How valuable time is to us may be gauged by the fact that the Enemy allows us so little of it. The majority of the human race dies in infancy; of the survivors, a good many die in youth. It is obvious that to Him human birth is important chiefly as the qualification for human death, and death solely as the gate to that other kind of life.

2. Inveterate: habitual, chronic.

3. Eugenics: the view that the genetic composition of a population can be improved through selective breeding. It eventually became associated with the practices of the Nazis in Germany.

4. Quoted from *Critique of Pure Reason* (1781), by German philosopher Immanuel Kant (1724–1804).

We are allowed to work only on a selected minority of the race, for what humans call a "normal life" is the exception. Apparently He wants some—but only a very few—of the human animals with which He is peopling Heaven to have had the experience of resisting us through an earthly life of sixty or seventy years. Well, there is our opportunity. The smaller it is, the better we must use it. Whatever you do, keep your patient as safe as you possibly can,

Your affectionate uncle
Screwtape

Letter 29

My dear Wormwood,

ow that it is certain the German humans will bombard your patient's town and that his duties will keep him in the thick of the danger, we must consider our policy. Are we to aim at cowardice—or at courage, with consequent pride—or at hatred of the Germans?

Well, I am afraid it is no good trying to make him brave. Our research department has not yet discovered (though success is hourly expected) how to produce *any* virtue. This is a serious handicap. To be greatly and effectively wicked a man needs some virtue. What would Attila[1] have been without his courage, or Shylock[2] without self-denial as regards the flesh? But as we cannot supply these qualities ourselves, we can only use them as supplied by the Enemy—and this

First published in *The Guardian* on November 14, 1941, with the title "Cowardice."

1. Attila was ruler of the Huns from 434 until 453. He was considered a ruthless and barbaric conqueror.

2. Shylock was a character in William Shakespeare's *The Merchant of Venice*. Shylock loans money to Antonio, requiring a "pound of flesh" if Antonio defaults.

means leaving Him a kind of foothold in those men whom, otherwise, we have made most securely our own. A very unsatisfactory arrangement, but, I trust, we shall one day learn to do better.

Hatred we can manage. The tension of human nerves during noise, danger, and fatigue, makes them prone to any violent emotion and it is only a question of guiding this susceptibility into the right channels. If conscience resists, muddle him. Let him say that he feels hatred not on his own behalf but on that of the women and children, and that a Christian is told to forgive his own, not other people's enemies. In other words let him consider himself sufficiently identified with the women and children to feel hatred on their behalf, but *not* sufficiently identified to regard their enemies as his own and therefore proper objects of forgiveness.

But hatred is best combined with Fear. Cowardice, alone of all the vices, is purely painful—horrible to anticipate, horrible to feel, horrible to remember; Hatred has its pleasures. It is therefore often the *compensation* by which a frightened man reimburses himself for the miseries of Fear. The more he fears, the more he will hate. And Hatred is also a great anodyne for shame. To make a deep wound in his charity, you should therefore first defeat his courage.

Now this is a ticklish business. We have made men proud of most vices, but not of cowardice. Whenever we have almost succeeded in doing so, the Enemy permits a war or an earthquake or some other calamity, and at once courage becomes so obviously lovely and important even in human eyes that all our work is undone, and there is still at least one vice of which they feel genuine shame. The danger of inducing cowardice in our patients, therefore, is lest we produce real self-knowledge and self-loathing with consequent repentance and humility. And in fact, in the last war, thousands of humans, by discovering their own cowardice, discovered the whole moral world for the first time.[3] In peace we can make many of them ignore good and evil entirely; in danger, the issue is forced upon them in a guise to which even we cannot blind them. There is here a cruel dilemma before us. If we promoted justice and charity among men, we should be playing directly into the Enemy's hands; but if we guide them to the opposite behaviour, this sooner or later

3. "My memories of the last war haunted my dreams for years. Military service, to be plain, includes the threat of every *temporal* evil; pain and death which is what we fear from sickness; isolation from those we love which is what we fear from exile; toil under arbitrary masters, injustice, humiliation which is what we fear from slavery; hunger, thirst, and exposure which is what we fear from poverty. I'm not a pacifist. If it's got to be it's got to be. But the flesh is weak and selfish and I think death would be much better than to live through another war." (Letter dated May 8, 1939, in *Collected Letters II*.)

produces (for He permits it to produce) a war or a revolution, and the undisguisable issue of cowardice or courage awakes thousands of men from moral stupor.

This, indeed, is probably one of the Enemy's motives for creating a dangerous world—a world in which moral issues really come to the point. He sees as well as you do that courage is not simply *one* of the virtues, but the form of every virtue at the testing point, which means, at the point of highest reality. A chastity or honesty or mercy, which yields to danger will be chaste or honest or merciful only on conditions. Pilate[4] was merciful till it became risky.

It is therefore possible to lose as much as we gain by making your man a coward; he may learn too much about himself! There is, of course, always the chance, not of chloroforming[5] the shame, but of aggravating it and producing Despair. This would be a great triumph. It would show that he had believed in, and accepted, the Enemy's forgiveness of his other sins only because he himself did not fully feel their sinfulness—that in respect of the one vice which he really understands in its full depth of dishonour he cannot seek, nor credit, the

4. Pilate, or Pontius Pilate, was the fifth prefect of Judea from 26 to 36. As the Roman ruler, Pilate heard the case of Jesus of Nazareth when he was accused of blasphemy and insurrection by the Jewish leaders. According to the Gospel accounts, Pilate was prepared to release Jesus until the Jewish leaders suggested that to do so would bring into question his loyalty to Caesar.

5. Chloroforming: causing unconsciousness, rendering useless.

Mercy. But I fear you have already let him get too far in the Enemy's school, and he knows that Despair is a greater sin than any of the sins which provoke it.

As to the actual technique of temptations to cowardice, not much need be said. The main point is that precautions have a tendency to increase fear. The precautions publicly enjoined on your patient, however, soon become a matter of routine and this effect disappears. What you must do is to keep running in his mind (side by side with the conscious intention of doing his duty) the vague idea of all sorts of things he can do or not do, *inside* the framework of the duty, which seem to make him a little safer. Get his mind off the simple rule ("I've got to stay here and do so-and-so") into a series of imaginary life lines ("If A happened—though I very much hope it won't—I could do B—and if the worst came to the worst, I could always do C"). Superstitions, if not recognised as such, can be awakened. The point is to keep him feeling that he has *something,* other than the Enemy and courage the Enemy supplies, to *fall back on,* so that what was intended to be a total commitment to duty becomes honeycombed all through with little unconscious reservations. By building up a series of imaginary expedients to prevent "the worst coming to the worst" you may produce, at that level of his will which he is not aware of, a determination that the worst *shall not* come to the worst. Then, at the moment of real terror, rush it out into his nerves and muscles and you may get the fatal act done before he knows what you're about. For remember, the *act* of cowardice is all that matters; the emotion of fear is, in itself, no sin and, though we enjoy it, does us no good,

Your affectionate uncle
Screwtape

Letter 30

My dear Wormwood,

First published in *The Guardian* on November 21, 1941.

 sometimes wonder whether you think you have been sent into the world for your own amusement. I gather, not from your miserably inadequate report but from that of the Infernal Police, that the patient's behaviour during the first raid has been the worst possible. He has been very frightened and thinks himself a great coward and therefore feels no pride; but he has done everything his duty demanded and perhaps a bit more. Against this disaster all you can produce on the credit side is a burst of ill temper with a dog that tripped him up, some excessive cigarette smoking, and the forgetting of a prayer. What is the use of whining to me about your difficulties? If you are proceeding on the Enemy's idea of "justice" and suggesting that your

1. Lewis explains his view of this in the 1961 preface (p. xxix).

2. Irremediable: impossible to cure or fix.

opportunities and intentions should be taken into account, then I am not sure that a charge of heresy does not lie against you. At any rate, you will soon find that the justice of Hell is purely realistic, and concerned only with results. Bring us back food, or be food yourself.[1]

The only constructive passage in your letter is where you say that you still expect good results from the patient's fatigue. That is well enough. But it won't fall into your hands. Fatigue *can* produce extreme gentleness, and quiet of mind, and even something like vision. If you have often seen men led by it into anger, malice, and impatience, that is because those men have had efficient tempters. The paradoxical thing is that moderate fatigue is a better soil for peevishness than absolute exhaustion. This depends partly on physical causes, but partly on something else. It is not fatigue simply as such that produces the anger, but unexpected demands on a man already tired. Whatever men expect they soon come to think they have a right to: the sense of disappointment can, with very little skill on our part, be turned into a sense of injury. It is after men have given in to the irremediable,[2] after they have despaired of relief and ceased to think even a half-hour ahead, that the dangers of humbled and gentle weariness begin. To produce the best results from the patient's fatigue, therefore, you must feed him with false hopes. Put into his mind plausible reasons for believing that the air-raid will not be repeated. Keep him comforting himself with the thought of how much he will enjoy his bed next night. Exaggerate the weariness by making him think it will soon be over; for men usually feel that a strain could have been endured no longer at the very moment when it is ending, or when they think it is ending. In this, as in the problem of cowardice, the thing to avoid is the total commitment. Whatever he *says,* let his inner resolution be not to bear whatever comes to him, but to bear it "for a reasonable period"—and let the reasonable period be shorter than the trial is likely to last. It need not be *much* shorter; in attacks on patience, chastity, and fortitude, the fun is to make the man yield just when (had he but known it) relief was almost in sight.

I do not know whether he is likely to meet the girl under conditions of strain or not. If he does, make full use of the fact that up to a certain point, fatigue makes women talk more and men talk less. Much secret resentment, even between lovers, can be raised from this.

Probably the scenes he is now witnessing will not provide material for an *intellectual* attack on his faith—your previous failures have put that out of your power. But there is a sort of attack on the emotions which can still be tried. It turns on making him *feel,* when first he sees human remains plastered on a wall, that this is "what the world is *really* like" and that all his religion has been a fantasy. You will notice that we have got them completely fogged about the meaning of the word "real." They tell each other, of some great spiritual experience, "All that *really* happened was that you heard some music in a lighted building"; here "real" means the bare physical facts, separated from the other elements in the experience they actually had. On the other hand, they will also say "It's all very well discussing that high dive as you sit here in an armchair, but wait till you get up there and see what it's *really* like": here "real" is being used in the opposite sense to mean, not the physical facts (which they know already while discussing the matter in armchairs) but the emotional effect those facts will have on a human consciousness. Either application of the word could be defended; but our business is to keep the two going at once so that the emotional value of the word "real" can be placed now on one side of the account, now on the other, as it happens to suit us. The general rule which we have now pretty well established among them is that in all experiences which can make them happier or better only the physical facts are "real" while the spiritual elements are "subjective"; in all experiences which can discourage or corrupt them the spiritual elements are the main reality and to ignore them is to be an escapist. Thus in birth the blood and pain are "real," the rejoicing a mere subjective point of view; in death, the terror and ugliness reveal what death "really means." The hatefulness of a hated person is "real"—in hatred you see men as they are, you are disillusioned; but the loveliness of a loved person is merely a subjective haze concealing a "real" core of sexual appetite or economic association. Wars and poverty are "really" horrible; peace and plenty are mere physical facts

This is the traditional rendering of the English proverb, though it has been popularly corrupted as "have one's cake and eat it too."

about which men happen to have certain sentiments. The creatures are always accusing one another of wanting "to eat the cake and have it";[3] but thanks to our labours they are more often in the predicament of paying for the cake and not eating it. Your patient, properly handled, will have no difficulty in regarding his emotion at the sight of human entrails as a revelation of Reality and his emotion at the sight of happy children or fair weather as mere sentiment,

Your affectionate uncle
Screwtape

Letter 31

My dear, my very dear, Wormwood, my poppet,[1] my pigsnie,[2]

ow mistakenly now that all is lost you come whimpering to ask me whether the terms of affection in which I address you meant nothing from the beginning. Far from it! Rest assured, my love for you and your love for me are as like as two peas. I have always desired you, as you (pitiful fool) desired me. The difference is that I am the stronger. I think they will give you to me now; or a bit of you. Love you? Why, yes. As dainty a morsel as ever I grew fat on.

You have let a soul slip through your fingers. The howl of sharpened famine for that loss re-echoes at this moment through all the levels of the Kingdom of Noise down to the very Throne itself. It makes me mad to think of it. How well I know what

First published in *The Guardian* on November 28, 1941.

1. Poppet is a term of endearment, a variation of "puppet," meaning a doll or small child.

2. Likely from Chaucer, pigsnie is a term of endearment akin to "darling." It may be a variation of "piga," which meant "young maid" in the Anglo-Saxon, or "pig's-eye," which also implied affection.

3. Tetter: any of a variety of skin diseases.

4. Lewis explains his view of purgatory, which he claimed to believe in, though not as a "Romish doctrine": "Our souls *demand* Purgatory, don't they? Would it not break the heart if God said to us, 'It is true, my son, that your breath smells and your rags drip with mud and slime, but we are charitable here and no one will upbraid you with these things, nor draw away from you. Enter into the joy'? Should we not reply, 'With submission, sir, and if there is no objection, I'd *rather* be cleaned first.' 'It may hurt, you know'—'Even so, sir.'" (*Letters to Malcolm,* chap. 20.)

happened at the instant when they snatched him from you! There was a sudden clearing of his eyes (was there not?) as he saw you for the first time, and recognised the part you had had in him and knew that you had it no longer. Just think (and let it be the beginning of your agony) what he felt at that moment; as if a scab had fallen from an old sore, as if he were emerging from a hideous, shell-like tetter,[3] as if he shuffled off for good and all a defiled, wet, clinging garment. By Hell, it is misery enough to see them in their mortal days taking off dirtied and uncomfortable clothes and splashing in hot water and giving little grunts of pleasure—stretching their eased limbs. What, then, of this final stripping, this complete cleansing?[4]

The more one thinks about it, the worse it becomes. He got through so easily! No gradual misgivings, no doctor's sentence, no nursing home, no operating theatre, no false hopes of life; sheer, instantaneous liberation. One moment it seemed to be all our world; the scream of bombs, the fall of houses, the stink and taste of high explosive on the lips and in the lungs, the feet burning with weariness, the heart cold with horrors, the brain reeling, the legs aching; next moment all this was gone, gone like a bad dream, never again to be of any account. Defeated, out-manoeuvred fool! Did you mark how naturally—as if he'd been born for it—the earth-born vermin entered the new life? How all his doubts became, in the twinkling of an eye, ridiculous? I know what the creature was saying to itself! "Yes. Of course. It always was like this. All horrors have followed the same course, getting worse and worse and forcing you into a kind of bottle-neck till, at the very moment when you thought you must be crushed, behold! you were out of the narrows and all was suddenly well. The extraction hurt more and more and then the tooth was out. The dream became a nightmare and then you woke. You die and die and then you are beyond death. How could I ever have doubted it?"

As he saw you, he also saw Them. I know how it was. You reeled back dizzy and blinded, more hurt by them than he had ever been by bombs. The degradation of it!—that this thing of earth and slime could stand upright and converse with spirits before whom you, a spirit, could only

5. The phrase "recognition made him free of their company" could be understood as "freed of their company," or that he could associate with them freely.

cower. Perhaps you had hoped that the awe and strangeness of it would dash his joy. But that is the cursed thing; the gods are strange to mortal eyes, and yet they are not strange. He had no faintest conception till that very hour of how they would look, and even doubted their existence. But when he saw them he knew that he had always known them and realized what part each one of them had played at many an hour in his life when he had supposed himself alone, so that now he could say to them, one by one, not "Who *are* you?" but "So it was you all the time." All that they were and said at this meeting woke memories. The dim consciousness of friends about him which had haunted his solitudes from infancy was now at last explained; that central music in every pure experience which had always just evaded memory was now at last recovered. Recognition made him free of their company[5] almost before the limbs of his corpse became quiet. Only you were left outside.

He saw not only Them; he saw Him. This animal, this thing begotten in a bed, could look on Him. What is blinding, suffocating fire to you, is now cool light to him, is clarity itself, and wears the form of a Man. You would like, if you could, to interpret the patient's prostration in the Presence, his self-abhorrence and utter knowledge of his sins (yes, Wormwood, a clearer knowledge even than yours) on the analogy of your own choking and paralysing sensations when you encounter the deadly air that breathes from the heart of Heaven. But it's all nonsense. Pains he may still have to encounter, but they *embrace* those pains. They would not barter them for any earthly pleasure. All the delights of sense, or heart, or intellect, with which you could once have tempted him, even the delights of virtue itself, now seem to him in comparison but as the half nauseous attractions of a raddled harlot would seem to a man who hears that his true beloved whom he has loved all his life and whom he had believed to be dead is alive and even now at his door. He is caught up into that world where pain and pleasure take on transfinite[6] values and all our arithmetic is dismayed. Once more, the inexplicable meets us.[7] Next to the curse of useless tempters like yourself the greatest curse upon us is the failure of our Intelligence Department. If

6. Transfinite: beyond any finite number.

7. Lewis muses upon, and describes, death in many of his works. Complementary to this description from Screwtape, we have another from Aslan in *The Last Battle* as he reveals to the Pevensie children their true condition: "'There *was* a railway accident,' said Aslan softly. 'Your father and mother and all of you are—as you used to call it in the Shadowlands—dead. The term is over: the holidays have begun. The dream is ended: this is the morning.' And as He spoke He no longer looked to them like a lion; but the things that began to happen after that were so great and beautiful that I cannot write them. And for us this is the end of all the stories, and we can most truly say that they all lived happily ever after. But for them it was only the beginning of the real story. All their life in this world and all their adventures in Narnia have only been the cover and the title page: now at last they were beginning Chapter One of the Great Story which no one on earth has read: which goes on forever: in which every chapter is better than the one before." (*Last Battle,* chap. 16.)

only we could find out what He is really up to! Alas, alas, that knowledge, in itself so hateful and mawkish a thing, should yet be necessary for Power! Sometimes I am almost in despair. All that sustains me is the conviction that our Realism, our rejection (in the face of all temptations) of all silly nonsense and claptrap, *must* win in the end. Meanwhile, I have you to settle with. Most truly do I sign myself.

Your increasingly and ravenously affectionate uncle
Screwtape

Screwtape Proposes a Toast

Screwtape Proposes a Toast

(The scene is in Hell at the annual dinner of the Tempters' Training College for young devils. The principal, Dr. Slubgob,[1] *has just proposed the health of the guests. Screwtape, a very experienced devil, who is the guest of honour, rises to reply:)*

Mr. Principal, your Imminence,[2] your Disgraces, my Thorns,[3] Shadies,[4] and Gentledevils:

t is customary on these occasions for the speaker to address himself chiefly to those among you who have just graduated and who will very soon be posted to official

On December 19, 1959, *Screwtape Proposes a Toast* appeared in *The Saturday Evening Post,* an American weekly magazine published between 1897 and 1969.

1. The college and Dr. Slubgob are often referenced in *The Screwtape Letters.*

2. "Imminence" is a play on the traditional "Eminence."

3. Thorns and thistles are associated with the work of devils, or a curse; reference the crown of thorns placed on Jesus Christ's head in the lead up to his crucifixion (Gospel of Matthew 27:29).

4. "Shadies" is a play on the ancient Roman use of the word "shades," or "ghosts."

Temptships on Earth. It is a custom I willingly obey. I well remember with what trepidation I awaited my own first appointment. I hope, and believe, that each one of you has the same uneasiness tonight. Your career is before you. Hell expects and demands that it should be—as mine was—one of unbroken success. If it is not, you know what awaits you.

I have no wish to reduce the wholesome and realistic element of terror, the unremitting anxiety, which must act as the lash and spur to your endeavours. How often you will envy the humans their faculty of sleep! Yet at the same time I would wish to put before you a moderately encouraging view of the strategical situation as a whole.

Your dreaded Principal has included in a speech full of points something like an apology for the banquet which he has set before us. Well, gentledevils, no one blames him. But it would be vain to deny that the human souls on whose anguish we have been feasting tonight were of pretty poor quality. Not all the most skillful cookery of our tormentors could make them better than insipid.

Oh, to get one's teeth again into a Farinata,[5] a Henry VIII,[6] or even a Hitler![7] There was real crackling there; something to crunch; a rage, an egotism, a cruelty only just less robust than our own. It put up a delicious resistance to being devoured. It warmed your inwards when you'd got it down.

Instead of this, what have we had to-night? There was a municipal authority with Graft[8] sauce. But personally I could not detect in him the flavour of a really passionate and brutal avarice such as delighted one in the great tycoons of the last century. Was he not unmistakably a Little Man—a creature of the petty rake-off pocketed with a petty joke in private and denied with the stalest platitudes in his public utterances—a grubby little nonentity who had drifted into corruption, only just realizing that he was corrupt, and chiefly because everyone else did it? Then there was the lukewarm Casserole of Adulterers. Could you find in it any trace of a fully inflamed, defiant, rebellious, insatiable lust? I couldn't. They all tasted to me like undersexed morons who had blundered or trickled into the wrong beds in automatic response to sexy advertisements,

5. Farinata degli Uberti (1212–1264) was an Italian aristocrat, military leader, and head of a Ghibelline (anti-papal) faction. He appeared in Dante's "Inferno" in *The Divine Comedy*.

6. Henry VIII (1491–1547) was king of England from 1509 to 1547. Because the pope would not recognize Henry's desire for annulment and divorce, Henry renounced the authority of the pope and established himself as the supreme head of the Church in England. He married six times.

7. Adolph Hitler (1889–1945) was the founder and leader of the Nazi Party in Germany. He was chancellor (1933–1945) and dictator of Nazi Germany (1934–1945). Through his leadership, millions of men, women, and children died at war or were exterminated.

8. Graft: corrupt use of money.

9. Valeria Messalina (25–48) was the third wife of the Roman emperor Claudius and known for her promiscuity and malevolence. She was executed for plotting against her husband.

10. Giacomo Casanova (1725–1798) was an Italian adventurer, author, and notorious womanizer—to such a degree that his name is now synonymous with a philanderer or sexually predatory man.

or to make themselves feel modern and emancipated, or to reassure themselves about their virility or their "normalcy," or even because they had nothing else to do. Frankly, to me who have tasted Messalina[9] and Casanova,[10] they were nauseating. The Trade Unionist stuffed with sedition was perhaps a shade better. He had done some real harm. He had, not quite unknowingly, worked for bloodshed, famine, and the extinction of liberty. Yes, in a way. But what a way! He thought of those ultimate objectives so little. Toeing the party line, self-importance, and above all mere routine, were what really dominated his life.

But now comes the point. Gastronomically, all this is deplorable. But I hope none of us puts gastronomy first. Is it not, in another and far more serious way, full of hope and promise?

Consider, first, the mere quantity. The quality may be wretched; but we never had souls (of a sort) in more abundance.

And then the triumph. We are tempted to say that such souls—or such residual puddles of what once was soul—are hardly worth damning. Yes, but the Enemy (for whatever inscrutable and perverse reason) thought them worth trying to save. Believe me, He did. You youngsters who have not yet been on active service have no idea with what labour, with what delicate skill, each of these miserable creatures was finally captured.

The difficulty lay in their very smallness and flabbiness. Here were vermin so muddled in mind, so passively responsive to environment, that it was very hard to raise them to that level of clarity and deliberateness at which mortal sin becomes possible. To raise them just enough; but not that fatal millimetre of "too much." For then, of course, all would possibly have been lost. They might have seen; they might have repented. On the other hand, if they had been raised too little, they would very possibly have qualified for Limbo,[11] as creatures suitable neither for Heaven nor for Hell; things that, having failed to make the grade, are allowed to sink into a more or less contented subhumanity forever.

In each individual choice of what the Enemy would call the "wrong" turning, such creatures are at first hardly, if at all, in a state of full spiritual responsibility. They do not understand either the source or the

11. Lewis explores the idea of limbo in *The Pilgrim's Regress*. In 1939, he wrote to a woman who took exception to his idea of limbo. He replied that he didn't "pretend to have any information on the fate of the virtuous unbeliever," but wryly suggested that "Residence in Limbo . . . is compatible with 'perishing everlastingly' and you'll find it quite jolly, for whereas Heaven is an acquired taste, Limbo is a place of 'perfect natural happiness.' In fact you may be able to realize your wish 'of attending with one's whole mind to the history of the human spirit.' There are grand libraries in Limbo, endless discussions, and no colds. There will be a faint melancholy because you'll all know that you have missed the bus, but that will provide a subject for poetry. The scenery is pleasant though tame. The climate endless autumn." (Letter dated April 5, 1939, in *Collected Letters II*.)

12. This is an echo from *The Screwtape Letters*. See "Letter 27" (p. 159).

13. See note 5 in "Letter 10" (p. 59) of *The Screwtape Letters*.

real character of the prohibitions they are breaking. Their consciousness hardly exists apart from the social atmosphere that surrounds them. And of course we have contrived that their very language should be all smudge and blur; what would be a *bribe* in someone else's profession is a *tip* or a *present* in theirs. The job of their Tempters was first, of course, to harden these choices of the Hellward roads into a habit by steady repetition. But then (and this was all important) to turn the habit into a principle—a principle the creature is prepared to defend. After that, all will go well. Conformity to the social environment, at first merely instinctive or even mechanical—how should a *jelly* not conform?—now becomes an unacknowledged creed or ideal of Togetherness or Being Like Folks. Mere ignorance of the law they break now turns into a vague theory about it—remember, they know no history[12]—a theory expressed by calling it *conventional* or *Puritan*[13] or *bourgeois* "morality." Thus gradually there comes to exist at the centre of the creature a hard, tight, settled core of resolution to go on being what it is, and even to resist moods that might tend to alter it. It is a very small core; not at all reflective (they are too ignorant) nor defiant (their emotional and imaginative poverty excludes that); almost, in its own way, prim and demure; like a pebble, or a very young cancer. But it will serve our turn. Here at last is a real and deliberate, though not fully articulate, rejection of what the Enemy calls Grace.[14]

These, then, are two welcome phenomena. First, the abundance of our captures: however tasteless our fare, we are in no danger of famine. And secondly, the triumph: the skill of our Tempters has never stood higher. But the third moral, which I have not yet drawn, is the most important of all.

The sort of souls on whose despair and ruin we have—well, I won't say feasted, but at any rate subsisted—tonight are increasing in numbers and will continue to increase. Our advices from Lower Command assure us that this is so; our directives warn us to orient all our tactics in view of this situation. The "great" sinners, those in whom vivid and genial passions have been pushed beyond the bounds and in whom an immense concentration of will has been devoted to objects which the Enemy abhors,

14. Of "Grace," Lewis states clearly, ". . . we are saved by grace, that in our flesh dwells no good thing, that we are, through and through, creatures not creators, derived beings, living not of ourselves but from Christ." (*Weight of Glory.*) This kind of grace, though, he differentiated from grace as God's spiritual provision for daily or momentary needs. In a letter from 1953, he wrote, "If and when a horror turns up you will then be given Grace to help you. I don't think one is usually given it in advance. 'Give us our daily bread' (not an annuity for life) applies to spiritual gifts too; the little *daily* support for the *daily* trial. Life has to be taken day by day and hour by hour." (Letter dated July 17, 1953, in *Collected Letters III.*)

15. Cerberus was a mythological three-headed hound that guarded the gates of the underworld and had a taste for live meat.

16. A reference to Jesus Christ.

will not disappear. But they will grow rarer. Our catches will be ever more numerous; but they will consist increasingly of trash—trash which we should once have thrown to Cerberus[15] and the hellhounds as unfit for diabolical consumption. And there are two things I want you to understand about this: First, that however depressing it may seem, it is really a change for the better. And secondly, I would draw your attention to the means by which it has been brought about.

It is a change for the better. The great (and toothsome) sinners are made out of the very same material as those horrible phenomena the great Saints. The virtual disappearance of such material may mean insipid meals for us. But is it not utter frustration and famine for the Enemy? He did not create the humans—He did not become one of them and die among them by torture[16]—in order to produce candidates for Limbo, "failed" humans. He wanted to make Saints; gods; things like Himself. Is the dullness of your present fare not a very small price to pay for the delicious knowledge that His whole great experiment is petering out? But not only that. As the great sinners grow fewer, and the majority lose all individuality, the great sinners become far more effective agents for us. Every dictator or even demagogue—almost every film star or crooner[17]—can now draw tens of thousands of the human sheep with him. They give themselves (what there is of them) to him; in him, to us. There may come a time when we shall have no need to bother about *individual* temptation at all, except for the few. Catch the bellwether,[18] and his whole flock comes after him.

But do you realize how we have succeeded in reducing so many of the human race to the level of ciphers?[19] This has not come about by accident. It has been our answer—and a magnificent answer it is—to one of the most serious challenges we ever had to face.

Let me recall to your minds what the human situation was in the latter half of the nineteenth century—the period at which I ceased to be a practising Tempter and was rewarded with an administrative post. The great movement towards liberty and equality among men had by then borne solid fruits and grown mature. Slavery had been abolished. The American War of Independence had been won. The French Revolution had succeeded. Religious toleration was almost

17. Crooner: a pop singer with a particular style of gentle sentimentality. American singer Bing Crosby (1903–1977) was the most famous of the crooners, though Lewis may be referring to most singing celebrities. Considering this was written on the eve of Beatlemania and what would later be called "the cult of personality," it seems particularly prophetic.

18. "Bellwether" is from the practice of putting a bell around the neck of a castrated ram (*wether* in Old English) that leads a flock of sheep. The bell would not only signal the sheep to follow, but indicate where the flock was for the shepherd. It later took on the meaning of a leader or someone who creates or influences trends or events.

19. Cipher: a person of no use, a nonentity.

20. Christian socialism was an ideology of social justice that viewed capitalism as a form of avarice and, as such, contrary to true Christian faith or practice.

everywhere on the increase. In that movement there had originally been many elements which were in our favour. Much Atheism, much Anti-clericalism, much envy and thirst for revenge, even some (rather absurd) attempts to revive Paganism, were mixed in it. It was not easy to determine what our own attitude should be. On the one hand it was a bitter blow to us—it still is—that any sort of men who had been hungry should be fed or any who had long worn chains should have them struck off. But on the other hand, there was in the movement so much rejection of faith, so much materialism, secularism, and hatred, that we felt we were bound to encourage it.

But by the latter part of the century the situation was much simpler, and also much more ominous. In the English sector (where I saw most of my frontline service) a horrible thing had happened. The Enemy, with His usual sleight of hand, had largely appropriated this progressive or liberalizing movement and perverted it to His own ends. Very little of its old anti-Christianity remained. The dangerous phenomenon called Christian Socialism[20] was rampant. Factory owners of the good old type who grew rich on sweated labour, instead of being assassinated by their workpeople—we could have used that—were being frowned upon by their own class. The rich were increasingly giving up their powers, not in the face of revolution and compulsion, but in obedience to their own consciences. As for the poor who benefited by this, they were behaving in a most disappointing fashion. Instead of using their new liberties—as we reasonably hoped and expected—for massacre, rape, and looting, or even for perpetual intoxication, they were perversely engaged in becoming cleaner, more orderly, more thrifty, better educated, and even more virtuous. Believe me, gentledevils, the threat of something like a really healthy state of society seemed then perfectly serious.

Thanks to Our Father Below, the threat was averted. Our counterattack was on two levels. On the deepest level our leaders contrived to call into full life an element which had been implicit in the movement from its earliest days. Hidden in the heart of this striving for Liberty there was also a deep hatred of personal freedom. That invaluable man Rousseau[21] first revealed it. In his perfect democracy, you remember,

21. Jean-Jacques Rousseau (1712–1778) was a philosopher, writer, and composer. Though he was a citizen of Geneva, Rousseau moved to Paris in 1742, where he eventually wrote philosophical books on a variety of subjects, including political science, social inequality, and rights. His writings and participation in the Jacobin Club influenced the French Revolution and also precipitated the Reign of Terror, which was marked by extensive violence and mass executions throughout France.

22. Georg Hegel (1770–1831) was a German philosopher and a driving force behind German idealism, particularly absolute idealism, throughout Europe.

23. The British had—and have— numerous laws and restrictions about cutting down trees, the use of the wood, and the addition of any kind of structure on an owner's property.

24. In *The Weight of Glory* Lewis explains, "I believe in political equality. But there are two opposite reasons for being a democrat. You may think all men so good that they deserve a share in the government of the commonwealth, and so wise that the commonwealth needs their advice. That is, in my opinion, the full, romantic doctrine of democracy. On the other hand, you may believe fallen men to be so wicked that not one of them can be trusted with any irresponsible power over his fellows. . . . That I believe to be the true ground of democracy."

only the state religion is permitted, slavery is restored, and the individual is told that he has really willed (though he didn't know it) whatever the Government tells him to do. From that starting point, via Hegel[22] (another indispensable propagandist on our side), we easily contrived both the Nazi and the Communist state. Even in England we were pretty successful. I heard the other day that in that country a man could not, without a permit, cut down his own tree with his own axe, make it into planks with his own saw, and use the planks to build a tool-shed in his own garden.[23]

Such was our counterattack on one level. You, who are mere beginners, will not be entrusted with work of that kind. You will be attached as Tempters to private persons. Against them, or through them, our counterattack takes a different form.

Democracy[24] is the word with which you must lead them by the nose. The good work which our philological experts have already done in the corruption of human language makes it unnecessary to warn you that they should never be allowed to give this word a clear and definable meaning. They won't. It will never occur to them that *democracy* is properly the name of a political system, even a system of voting, and that this has only the most remote and tenuous connection with what you are trying to sell them. Nor of course must they ever be allowed to raise Aristotle's[25] question: whether "democratic behaviour" means the behaviour that democracies like or the behaviour that will preserve a democracy. For if they did, it could hardly fail to occur to them that these need not be the same.

You are to use the word purely as an incantation; if you like, purely for its selling power. It is a name they venerate. And of course it is connected with the political ideal that men should be equally treated. You then make a stealthy transition in their minds from this political ideal to a factual belief that all men *are* equal. Especially the man you are working on. As a result you can use the word *democracy* to sanction in his thought the most degrading (and also the least enjoyable) of all human feelings. You can get him to practise, not only without shame but with a positive glow of self-approval, conduct which, if undefended by the magic word, would be universally derided.

25. Aristotle (384–322 BC) was a Greek philosopher, scientist, and teacher, and one of the most influential men in Western civilization.

The feeling I mean is of course that which prompts a man to say *I'm as good as you*.

The first and most obvious advantage is that you thus induce him to enthrone at the centre of his life a good solid, resounding lie. I don't mean merely that his statement is false in fact, that he is no more equal to everyone he meets in kindness, honesty, and good sense than in height or waist measurement. I mean that he does not believe it himself. No man who says *I'm as good as you* believes it. He would not say it if he did. The St. Bernard never says it to the toy dog, nor the scholar to the dunce, nor the employable to the bum, nor the pretty woman to the plain. The claim to equality, outside the strictly political field, is made only by those who feel themselves to be in some way inferior. What it expresses is precisely the itching, smarting, writhing awareness of an inferiority which the patient refuses to accept.

And therefore resents. Yes, and therefore resents every kind of superiority in others; denigrates it; wishes its annihilation. Presently he suspects every mere difference of being a claim to superiority. No one must be different from himself in voice, clothes, manners, recreations, choice of food: "Here is someone who speaks English rather more clearly and euphoniously than I—it must be a vile, upstage, la-di-da affectation. Here's a fellow who says he doesn't like hot dogs—thinks himself too good for them, no doubt. Here's a man who hasn't turned on the jukebox—he's one of those goddam highbrows and is doing it to show off. If they were honest-to-God all-right Joes they'd be like me. They've no business to be different. It's undemocratic."

Now, this useful phenomenon is in itself by no means new. Under the name of Envy it has been known to the humans for thousands of years. But hitherto they always regarded it as the most odious, and also the most comical, of vices. Those who were aware of feeling it felt it with shame; those who were not gave it no quarter in others. The delightful novelty of the present situation is that you can sanction it—make it respectable and even laudable—by the incantatory use of the word *democratic*.

Under the influence of this incantation those who are in any or every way inferior can labour more wholeheartedly and successfully than ever before to pull down

26. Minx: a flirtatious young woman.

27. Cranks: grouches or grumpy people, eccentrics.

everyone else to their own level. But that is not all. Under the same influence, those who come, or could come, nearer to a full humanity, actually draw back from it for fear of being undemocratic. I am credibly informed that young humans now sometimes suppress an incipient taste for classical music or good literature because it might prevent their Being Like Folks; that people who would really wish to be—and are offered the Grace which would enable them to be—honest, chaste, or temperate refuse it. To accept might make them Different, might offend against the Way of Life, take them out of Togetherness, impair their Integration with the Group. They might (horror of horrors!) become individuals.

All is summed up in the prayer which a young female human is said to have uttered recently: "O God, make me a normal twentieth century girl!" Thanks to our labours, this will mean increasingly, "Make me a minx,[26] a moron, and a parasite."

Meanwhile, as a delightful by-product, the few (fewer every day) who will not be made Normal and Regular and Like Folks and Integrated increasingly tend to become in reality the prigs and cranks[27] which the rabble would in any case have believed them to be. For suspicion often creates what it suspects. ("Since, whatever I do, the neighbours are going to think me a witch, or a Communist agent, I might as well be hanged for a sheep as a lamb,[28] and become one in reality.") As a result we now have an intelligentsia which, though very small, is very useful to the cause of Hell.

But that is a mere by-product. What I want to fix your attention on is the vast, overall movement towards the discrediting, and finally the elimination, of every kind of human excellence—moral, cultural, social, or intellectual. And is it not pretty to notice how "democracy" (in the incantatory sense) is now doing for us the work that was once done by the most ancient Dictatorships, and by the same methods? You remember how one of the Greek Dictators (they called them "tyrants" then) sent an envoy to another Dictator to ask his advice about the principles of government. The second Dictator led the envoy into a field of grain, and there he snicked off with his cane the top of every stalk that rose an inch or so above the general level. The moral was plain. Allow no preeminence among your subjects. Let

28. "Hanged for a sheep as a lamb" is an expression suggesting that, if I'm going to be punished anyway, I may as well commit the greater sin or crime.

no man live who is wiser or better or more famous or even handsomer than the mass. Cut them all down to a level: all slaves, all ciphers, all nobodies. All equals. Thus Tyrants could practise, in a sense, "democracy." But now "democracy" can do the same work without any tyranny other than her own. No one need now go through the field with a cane. The little stalks will now of themselves bite the tops off the big ones. The big ones are beginning to bite off their own in their desire to Be Like Stalks.

I have said that to secure the damnation of these little souls, these creatures that have almost ceased to be individual, is a laborious and tricky work. But if proper pains and skill are expended, you can be fairly confident of the result. The great sinners seem easier to catch. But then they are incalculable. After you have played them for seventy years, the Enemy may snatch them from your claws in the seventy-first. They are capable, you see, of real repentance. They are conscious of real guilt. They are, if things take the wrong turn, as ready to defy the social pressures around them for the Enemy's sake as they were to defy them for ours. It is in some ways more troublesome to track and swat an evasive wasp than to shoot, at close range, a wild elephant. But the elephant is more troublesome if you miss.

My own experience, as I have said, was mainly on the English sector, and I still get more news from it than from any other. It may be that what I am now going to say will not apply so fully to the sectors in which some of you may be operating. But you can make the necessary adjustments when you get there. Some application it will almost certainly have. If it has too little, you must labour to make the country you are dealing with more like what England already is.

In that promising land the spirit of *I'm as good as you* has already become something more than a generally social influence. It begins to work itself into their educational system. How far its operations there have gone at the present moment, I should not like to say with certainty. Nor does it matter. Once you have grasped the tendency, you can easily predict its future developments; especially as we ourselves will play our part in the developing. The basic principle of the new education is to be that dunces and idlers must not be made to feel inferior to intelligent and industrious pupils. That would

29. Parity of esteem in British education was an effort to bring equality to all classes in fields of learning, though the effort eventually led to practices just as Lewis, via Screwtape, describes here.

30. Originally, the name Beelzebub was applied to an ancient Philistine god, but it came to be connected with the devil.

be "undemocratic." These differences between the pupils—for they are obviously and nakedly *individual* differences—must be disguised. This can be done on various levels. At universities, examinations must be framed so that nearly all the students get good marks. Entrance examinations must be framed so that all, or nearly all, citizens can go to universities, whether they have any power (or wish) to profit by higher education or not. At schools, the children who are too stupid or lazy to learn languages and mathematics and elementary science can be set to doing the things that children used to do in their spare time. Let them, for example, make mud-pies and call it modelling. But all the time there must be no faintest hint that they are inferior to the children who are at work. Whatever nonsense they are engaged in must have—I believe the English already use the phrase—"parity of esteem."[29] An even more drastic scheme is not impossible. Children who are fit to proceed to a higher class may be artificially kept back, because the others would get a *trauma*—Beelzebub,[30] what a useful word!—by being left behind. The bright pupil thus remains democratically fettered to his own age group throughout his school career, and a boy who would be capable of tackling Aeschylus[31] or Dante[32] sits listening to his coeval's[33] attempts to spell out A CAT SAT ON A MAT.

In a word, we may reasonably hope for the virtual abolition of education when *I'm as good as you* has fully had its way. All incentives to learn and all penalties for not learning will vanish. The few who might want to learn will be prevented; who are they to overtop their fellows? And anyway the teachers—or should I say, nurses?—will be far too busy reassuring the dunces and patting them on the back to waste any time on real teaching. We shall no longer have to plan and toil to spread imperturbable conceit and incurable ignorance among men. The little vermin themselves will do it for us.

Of course, this would not follow unless all education became state education. But it will. That is part of the same movement. Penal taxes, designed for that purpose, are liquidating the Middle Class, the class who were prepared to save and spend and make sacrifices in order to have their children privately educated. The removal of this class,

31. Aeschylus (c. 524–c. 455 BC) was a Greek playwright.

32. See note 21 in the preface from the 1961 edition (p. xxxv).

33. Coeval: someone of the same age, a classmate.

34. John Henry Newman wryly noted that "despotisms require great monarchs . . . constitutions jog on without them," which may have been the basis for the quoted remark from the mysterious "English politician."

besides linking up with the abolition of education, is, fortunately, an inevitable effect of the spirit that says *I'm as good as you.* This was, after all, the social group which gave to the humans the overwhelming majority of their scientists, physicians, philosophers, theologians, poets, artists, composers, architects, jurists, and administrators. If ever there was a bunch of tall stalks that needed their tops knocked off, it was surely they. As an English politician remarked not long ago, "A democracy does not want great men."[34]

It would be idle to ask of such a creature whether by *want* it meant "need" or "like." But you had better be clear. For here Aristotle's question comes up again.

We, in Hell, would welcome the disappearance of democracy in the strict sense of that word, the political arrangement so called. Like all forms of government, it often works to our advantage, but on the whole less often than other forms. And what we must realize is that "democracy" in the diabolical sense (*I'm as good as you,* Being like Folks, Togetherness) is the finest instrument we could possibly have for extirpating[35] political democracies from the face of the earth.

For "democracy" or the "democratic spirit" (diabolical sense) leads to a nation without great men, a nation mainly of sub-literates, full of the cocksureness[36] which flattery breeds on ignorance, and quick to snarl or whimper at the first hint of criticism. And that is what Hell wishes every democratic people to be. For when such a nation meets in conflict a nation where children have been made to work at school, where talent is placed in high posts, and where the ignorant mass are allowed no say at all in public affairs, only one result is possible.

One Democracy was surprised lately when it found that Russia had got ahead of it in science.[37] What a delicious specimen of human blindness! If the whole tendency of their society is opposed to every sort of excellence, why did they expect their scientists to excel?

It is our function to encourage the behaviour, the manners, the whole attitude of mind, which democracies naturally like and enjoy, because these are the very things

35. Extirpating: completely removing.

36. Cocksureness: arrogant certainty, overconfidence.

37. A reference to the successful launch of a spaceship—the *Sputnik I*—by the Soviet Union on October 4, 1957.

which, if unchecked, will destroy democracy. You would almost wonder that even humans don't see it themselves. Even if they don't read Aristotle (that would be undemocratic) you would have thought the French Revolution would have taught them that the behaviour aristocrats naturally like is not the behaviour that preserves aristocracy. They might then have applied the same principle to all forms of government.

But I would not end on that note. I would not—Hell forbid!—encourage in your own minds that delusion which you must carefully foster in the minds of your human victims. I mean the delusion that the fate of nations is *in itself* more important than that of individual souls. The overthrow of free peoples and the multiplication of slave states are for us a means (besides, of course, being fun); but the real end is the destruction of individuals. For only individuals can be saved or damned, can become sons of the Enemy or food for us. The ultimate value, for us, of any revolution, war, or famine lies in the individual anguish, treachery, hatred, rage, and despair which it may produce. *I'm as good as you* is a useful means for the destruction of democratic societies. But it has a far deeper value as an end in itself, as a state of mind which, necessarily excluding humility, charity, contentment, and all the pleasures of gratitude or admiration, turns a human being away from almost every road which might finally lead him to Heaven.

But now for the pleasantest part of my duty. It falls to my lot to propose on behalf of the guests the health of Principal Slubgob and the Tempters' Training College. Fill your glasses. What is this I see? What is this delicious bouquet I inhale? Can it be? Mr. Principal, I unsay all my hard words about the dinner. I see, and smell, that even under wartime conditions the College cellar still has a few dozen of sound old vintage *Pharisee*.[38] Well, well, well. This is like old times. Hold it beneath your nostrils for a moment, gentledevils. Hold it up to the light. Look at those fiery streaks that writhe and tangle in its dark heart, as if they were contending. And so they are. You know how this wine is blended? Different types of Pharisee have been harvested, trodden, and fermented together to produce its subtle flavour. Types that were most antagonistic to one another on Earth. Some were all rules and relics[39] and rosaries;[40] others were all drab clothes,

38. In Ancient Israel, the pharisees were a powerful religious group. "Pharisee" later expanded to include any person who was self-righteous or hypocritical.

39. Relics, in this context, may refer to any valued historical item, a specifically religious item, or a part of the body of a saint carefully preserved.

40. Rosaries—from a Latin word meaning "rose garden"—were originally a garland of roses used as an aid to devotional prayers, later replaced by a string of beads. They are used primarily in the Catholic Church.

41. Lewis is returning to the subject of factions, as explored in "Letter 7" of *The Screwtape Letters* (p. 39).

42. A litany is a prayer used during worship in which a series of petitions are recited by a leader with fixed responses from the congregation. It has also come to mean a long and repetitious list.

long faces, and petty traditional abstinences from wine or cards or the theatre. Both had in common their self-righteousness and the almost infinite distance between their actual outlook and anything the Enemy really is or commands.[41] The wickedness of other religions was the really live doctrine in the religion of each; slander was its gospel and denigration its litany.[42] How they hated each other up there where the sun shone! How much more they hate each other now that they are forever conjoined but not reconciled. Their astonishment, their resentment, at the combination, the festering of their eternally impenitent spite, passing into our spiritual digestion, will work like fire. Dark fire. All said and done, my friends, it will be an ill day for us if what most humans mean by "religion" ever vanishes from the Earth. It can still send us the truly delicious sins. The fine flower of unholiness can grow only in the close neighbourhood of the Holy. Nowhere do we tempt so successfully as on the very steps of the altar.

Your Imminence, your Disgraces, my Thorns, Shadies, and Gentledevils: I give you the toast of—Principal Slubgob and the College!

Acknowledgments

A work like this would have been far more daunting had it not been for the remarkable encouragement and help of:

Doug Gresham, for his ongoing inspiration.

Devin Brown, professor of English at Asbury College, for his insights and expertise. He brought fresh ideas to many of the notes.

Kurt Bruner for his support, friendship and observations about Lewis over the years.

Elizabeth McCusker for her keen eye and helpful enthusiasm. And to Thomas and Eleanor for their understanding of, and patience with, Dad and what he does for a living.

To David Brawn for getting the project started and Mickey Maudlin for clearing the way.

Any resemblance between the names and characters used by C. S. Lewis in *The Screwtape Letters* and persons living or dead is to be expected.

C. S. Lewis's Ten Favorite Books

On June 6, 1962, *Christian Century* published a list
by C. S. Lewis of the ten books that influenced him
the most. They are, as he listed them:

Phantastes by George MacDonald

The Everlasting Man by G. K. Chesterton

The Aeneid by Virgil

The Temple by George Herbert

The Prelude by William Wordsworth

The Idea of the Holy by Rudolph Otto

The Consolation of Philosophy by Boethius

The Life of Samuel Johnson by James Boswell

Descent into Hell by Charles Williams

Theism and Humanism by Arthur James Balfour

Further Reading

To create an annotated edition like this, the author is indebted to many others who have researched and explored *The Screwtape Letters*. Here is a short list of works consulted or recommended.

BOOKS

Devin Brown. *Inside Narnia: A Guide to Exploring the Lion, the Witch, and the Wardrobe.* Grand Rapids, MI: Baker Books, 2005.

Bruce L. Edwards. *C. S. Lewis: Life, Works, and Legacy.* 4 volumes. Westport, CT: Praeger Perspectives, 2007.

Douglas Gresham. *Lenten Lands: My Childhood with Joy Davidman and C. S. Lewis.* New York: Macmillan, 1988.

Alan Jacobs. *The Narnian: The Life and Imagination of C. S. Lewis.* San Francisco: HarperCollins, 2005.

Clyde S. Kilby. *The Christian World of C. S. Lewis.* Grand Rapids, MI: W. B. Eerdmans, 1964.

Roger Lancelyn Green and Walter Hooper. *C. S. Lewis: A Biography.* London: Collins, 1974.

C. S. Lewis. *A Mind Awake: An Anthology of C. S. Lewis.* Edited by Clyde S. Kilby. London: Geoffrey Bles, 1968.

C. S. Lewis. *C. S. Lewis at the Breakfast Table and Other Reminiscences.* Edited by James T. Como. London: Collins, 1979.

C. S. Lewis. *The C. S. Lewis Bible.* New Revised Standard Version. New York: HarperCollins, 2010.

C. S. Lewis. *The Quotable Lewis.* Edited by Wayne Martindale and Jerry Root. Wheaton, IL: Tyndale House, 1989.

C. S. Lewis. *Reading the Classics with C. S. Lewis.* Edited by Thomas L. Martin. Grand Rapids, MI: Baker Books, 2000.

Kathryn Ann Lindskoog. *C. S. Lewis: Mere Christian.* Wheaton, IL: Harold Shaw, 1987.

Wayne Martindale, Jerry Root, and Linda Washington. *The Soul of C. S. Lewis.* Carol Stream, IL: Tyndale House, 2010.

John Milton. *The Annotated Milton: Complete English Poems.* Edited and with annotations lexical, syntactic, prosodic, and referential by Burton Raffel. New York: Bantam Books, 1999.

Joseph Pearce. *C. S. Lewis and the Catholic Church.* San Francisco: Ignatius Press, 2003.

Justin Philips. *C. S. Lewis in a Time of War.* San Francisco: HarperCollins, 2002. (Published in the UK as *C. S. Lewis at the BBC.*)

George Sayer. *Jack: C. S. Lewis and His Times.* London: Macmillan, 1988.

WEBSITES

C. S. Lewis (www.cslewis.com), established and
    maintained by HarperOne.
C. S. Lewis Foundation (www.cslewis.org),
    established and maintained by the C. S. Lewis
    Foundation, founded by Stan Mattson.
Into the Wardrobe: A C. S. Lewis Website
    (www.cslewis.drzeus.net), established in 1994
    by John Visser.
Lewisiana (www.lewisiana.nl), established by
    Arend Smilde.
Wikipedia (www.wikipedia.org), formally
    launched in 2001 by Jimmy Wales and Larry
    Sanger.